THE TEMPEST

THE TEMPEST

JULIE TAYMOR
ADAPTED FROM THE PLAY BY
WILLIAM SHAKESPEARE

FOREWORD BY JONATHAN BATE
INTRODUCTION BY JULIE TAYMOR

CONTENTS

ENTER ARIEL, INVISIBLE

Jonathan Bate

IN 1623, SEVEN YEARS AFTER WILLIAM SHAKESPEARE'S DEATH, his collected plays were published for the first time in the magnificent large-format volume known as the First Folio. The book was prepared for the press by the people who knew Shakespeare and his work more intimately than anyone else: John Hemmings and Henry Condell, the leading members of his acting company the King's Men, and Ben Jonson, his friend, rival, and fellow dramatist.

They decided to begin the book not with one of the great tragedies—*Hamlet*, *Othello,* or *King Lear*—but with a magical comedy: *The Tempest*. Shorter than many of the other plays, it was more tightly constructed (and would be more accurately printed) than any other. Most unusually for the plays of Shakespeare's time, it followed the ancient principle of dramatic unity: there is a single location and a single objective to the plot. What is more, the action comes close to working in real time: the story unfolds in a single afternoon between the hours of two and six o'clock.

The central character is a magician who practices "potent art," who commands over "actors" and puts on a play. At some level, Prospero is Shakespeare. And at some level, the island on which the action takes place is the performance space: the theater.

This extreme artfulness and these connections to the process of making drama may explain why *The Tempest* stands in pride of place at the head of the Folio: it is the showcase for Shakespeare's own art. Nearly two hundred years after his death, when biographers and critics began linking his life to his work, it was discovered that *The Tempest*, written in 1611, was also his last solo-authored play. It could thus be read as his valediction, a bravura farewell to the stage. As Prospero retires to Milan and thinks on his grave, so Shakespeare, it was said, retired to Stratford-upon-Avon in order to think on his.

In reality, though, Shakespeare kept one foot in the theater world. He collaborated on three further plays with John Fletcher, grooming the younger dramatist to take over his role as in-house playwright for the King's Men. And he bought a gatehouse close by the Blackfriars theater. The link with the Blackfriars is crucial for an understanding of the kind of play that *The Tempest* is.

Shakespeare's early works, such as *Titus*, Julie Taymor's previous Shakespearean movie, were written for the outdoor Rose theater. His middle-period triumphs, such as *Macbeth* in tragedy, *Twelfth Night* in comedy, and *Henry V* in history, were written for the outdoor Globe theater. One problem with an outdoor theater—especially in rainy old London town—is the weather. Another is that your opportunities for special effects and visual conjuring tricks are limited: you are not in control of the light, you have limited scope for flying, and the ambient noise of street and river outside may drown out your sound effects and your quiet music.

It was in order to overcome these challenges that in 1596 James Burbage, the theatrical entrepreneur who presided over Shakespeare's company, purchased a disused monastery called the Blackfriars, in the heart of London's legal district where there was a strong captive audience of smart young people with disposable income. At great expense, Burbage converted the old refectory into an indoor venue for winter theatrical productions. But wealthy local residents objected: they didn't want raffish theater types and late-night noise in their backyard. Unable to bring his theater company across the river, Burbage leased the premises out to a company of boy players for more low-key private performances. But then in 1608 the boys' company was disbanded, and Burbage's sons, Richard (Shakespeare's closest friend, the greatest actor England had ever seen, the original Romeo, Hamlet, Othello, and Lear) and Cuthbert (producer and business manager), formed a syndicate to manage the Blackfriars playhouse, together with five other members of the King's Men, including Hemmings, Condell, and Shakespeare himself.

At last they had a winter home, a regular indoor venue. From 1608, Shakespeare's style changed noticeably to accommodate this. The scenic structure of his plays had hitherto been extremely fluid, but now he needed to introduce act breaks, to allow the action to pause while the candles that lit the stage were changed, to the accompaniment of music. With a smaller and quieter audience, he could also write more complicated and experimental verse. And above all, he could start experimenting with special effects. This was the period when Ben Jonson and Inigo Jones were pioneering a new theater of elaborate visual and musical spectacle in the form known as the court masque— an all-singing, all-dancing genre in which we see the origins of the opera and ultimately the musical. Shakespeare incorporates a wedding masque into the action of *The Tempest,* but the influence of the new stage technology made possible by the indoor space goes further than this. The script includes stage directions that are unprecedented in the demands they make upon the art of dramatic magic:

> A tempestuous noise of thunder and lightning heard.
> Enter Mariners, wet.
> A confused noise within.
> Enter Ariel, like a water-nymph.
> Ariel, invisible, playing and singing.
> Solemn and strange music: and Prospero on the top, invisible.
> Enter several strange shapes, bringing in a banquet, and dance

> about it with gentle actions of salutations.
> Enter Ariel, like a harpy: claps his wings upon the table, and, with a quaint device, the banquet vanishes.
> Enter diverse spirits, in shape of dogs and hounds, hunting them about.
> They all enter the circle which Prospero had made, and there stand charmed.
> Here Prospero discovers Ferdinand and Miranda playing at chess.

The sound of a storm. A character who is at once visible and invisible. A charmed circle. Strangely shaped spirits: water nymph, harpy, dogs, and hounds. The realization of such effects on stage would have required many a "quaint device" of the kind that depended on the enclosed, controlled, dimly lit space of the indoor theater. We know that *The Tempest* was performed at the royal court—another indoor venue—in 1611 and again in 1613. The King's Men continued to play an outdoor summer season at the Globe in the years after they had obtained the Blackfriars as their indoor winter house, but there is no evidence that *The Tempest* was ever played at the Globe. It may have been the single Shakespeare play that was written exclusively for an indoor, high-tech theater.

The storm must seem real if we are to believe in Prospero's power to control the elements. Ariel must really seem to fly and to be meta-morphosed into all manner of forms if we are to believe in Prospero's power to control the spirits of the air. *The Tempest* is Shakespeare's great drama of *special effects*.

But—and again this is a consequence of the move to the intimate space of the Blackfriars (its capacity a few hundred, close packed in a hall, as opposed to several thousand in the yard and galleries of the great Globe itself)—it is also his great drama of *close up*. A parent talking intimately to a child. A spirit that whispers like a conscience. Two young lovers exploring new sensations. You need to bring the camera in tight, to listen attentively to the poetry, to see the emotions played on the faces.

In all this, both the magic of the special effects and the intimacy of the dialogue, *The Tempest* is crying out for a new medium. For film.

Shakespeare's language ravishes the ears: "the fringèd curtains of thine eye advance," "the dark backward and abysm of time," "the isle is full of noises, / Sounds and sweet airs, that give delight and hurt not." In his theater, the costumes would have ravished the eyes, but the creation of the surrounding environment of the action—the fertile island, the stormy sea, the magician's laboratory—would have been left to the audience's imagination. The technology of modern production, by contrast, has the capacity to create visual images that do justice to Shakespeare's verbal imagery.

Julie Taymor knows all this instinctively. In 1986, aged just thirty-three, she directed *The Tempest* for the Theater for a New Audience in New York. Gossamer light sculptures by the artist Caterina Bertolotto transformed the space of the stage into the magical island. Taymor's collaborator, Elliot Goldenthal, provided a complete musical score to complement the action and the poetry. Ariel's unreality was represented by his being a "puppet," performed in the manner of the Japanese Bunraku—where the operator is visible to the audience: when Ariel was freed, so was the puppeteer/actress. Simple but beautiful effects brought Shakespearean language into three dimensions: "The cloud-capped towers, the gorgeous palaces" became a sand castle dissolving in the rain—as in the stunning opening image of the movie.

A movie is a different medium from a stage-play, but Taymor's starting point is the same. She looks for the essence of the original work of art and then finds ways of matching it to the technical possibilities—the magic—of the new medium.

There is always a degree of serendipity in such a process. Taymor wanted to cast Ben Whishaw as Ariel, but he was not available for the shoot in Hawaii. No matter: a virtue could be made of the necessity. "*Enter Ariel, invisible*": he is a spirit, much of the time the other characters cannot see him, in some sense he is *not there*. What could be more fitting than for him not to be there on the shoot? Taymor filmed him alone against a green screen and then suffused his magical transformations into the environment of the island *in the editing suite*. "Where should this music be? I'th'air or th'earth?" asks Ferdinand, when he hears the invisible Ariel singing "Come unto these yellow sands" (here transformed to "darkened sands," in acknowledgment of the island's dark volcanic soil). Thanks to the magic of digital manipulation, combined with in-camera photographic techniques and specialized makeup, we see Ariel both in the air and in the earth—just as we see him become a harpy, a hound, a water nymph, a spirit who can "flame amazement" and "divide" himself "in many places."

THE RELATIONSHIP BETWEEN PROSPERO and his servant-spirit Ariel is at the heart of the play. Their encounters move rapidly between affection ("Do you love me, master? No?") and command ("Go bring the rabble"). Taymor catches these shifts as we see Ariel in intimate close-up with Prospera (in the play's intriguing gender switch) one moment, shooting through the air and multiplying himself the next. Ultimately, the human relationship comes to seem more important than the technical wizardry. That, after all, is the narrative arc of the play. The crucial encounter in which Ariel the spirit teaches Prospera the magician what it means to be human was filmed after the main shoot, with Helen Mirren and Whishaw face to face. If you saw your

penitent enemies, says Ariel, "your affections / Would become tender." Prospera is amazed at this insight: "Dost thou think so, spirit?" "Mine would, master, *were I human*," responds Ariel, eliciting the great speech of self-recognition and renunciation:

> And mine shall.
> Hast thou, which art but air, a touch, a feeling
> Of their afflictions, and shall not myself,
> One of their kind, be kindlier moved than thou art?
> Though with their high wrongs I am struck to th' quick,
> Yet with my nobler reason 'gainst my fury
> Do I take part: the rarer action is
> In virtue than in vengeance. They being penitent,
> The sole drift of my purpose doth extend
> Not a frown further. Go release them, Ariel:
> My charms I'll break, their senses I'll restore,
> And they shall be themselves.

The closeness of this exchange, the crux of the play, is intensified by the contrast between its absolute intimacy and the way that in earlier encounters the relationship of master and servant, the sense in which Prospera is a stage director and Ariel her actor, has been a barrier to love.

GREAT WORKS OF ART SURVIVE by means of the cultural equivalent of the Darwinian principle of adaptation. The key to evolution is the survival of the fittest: species that adapt to changing environmental circumstances will survive, while those that do not become extinct. As with natural selection, the quality that makes a really successful and enduring cultural artifact is the capacity to change in response to new environments, new cultural circumstances. Certain works of art are able to speak in new ways to later generations because they are very successful at plugging into the archetypal struggles that make up the human condition or because they give distinctive form to the enduring narratives that make us habitual storytellers and listeners to stories.

Shakespeare wrote for a theater where women did not perform in major roles on the stage, and yet when women did begin to perform, actresses found that some of the most supremely rewarding roles in the canon of western drama were those that Shakespeare originally wrote for teenage male apprentice actors. When the London playhouses were reopened during the Restoration years of the 1660s after their long closure during the English civil war and republican era, there were wholly new conditions (actresses, proscenium arches, and naturalistic scenery), so Shakespeare's plays were manipulated and reworked to speak to the concerns of the new age. And that's a story that has continued for another three and a half centuries. The work of adaptation will often involve an element of radical reinterpretation. Typically in the seventeenth and eighteenth centuries that process actually took the form of rewriting the words. In the twentieth and twenty-first centuries, more often than not the original words stay the same, but the director's interpretation of the story and the characters creates a radically new spin, and the plays somehow seem to be robust enough to withstand this. Shakespeare can be as powerful in the media of which he could not have dreamed—movie, DVD, down-load—as he always has been in those which he knew (the book, the platform stage, the auditorium in which actor and audience share the same space).

The problem with *The Tempest* for the Restoration theater in which Shakespeare had to be adapted for the benefit of that new cultural species, the *actress*, was that the text had only a single female part, that of Miranda. So it was that the leading dramatists of the day, John Dryden and William Davenant, adapted it into *The Tempest, or The Enchanted Island*, which premiered in London in 1667. In order to provide employment for the star actresses, who were one of the main reasons people went to the theater, Dryden and Davenant added several new parts, among them Dorinda, a second daughter for Prospero, who falls in love with another new character, a man called Hippolito who has never seen a woman (a nice parallel with Miranda, the woman who has never seen a man with the exception of her father, and the figure of Caliban, who is not perceived as a "normal" man). In addition, Ariel is given a spirit girlfriend called Milcha, and Caliban is provided with a sister. A few years later, a rival dramatist, Thomas Shadwell, turned the play into something akin to an opera, which held the stage for a century and half. Only in 1838 was there a revival of the Shakespearean original.

All this goes to show that it is neither new nor in any sense shocking for Julie Taymor to have casted Helen Mirren as Prospero. She is following in the venerable tradition of Dryden and Davenant by giving the role to a great actor who happens to be female. In 2000, another great female actor, Vanessa Redgrave, was cast as Prospero at Shakespeare's restored Globe Theatre in London. She played him as a man. Taymor has made the more interesting, more Davenantesque choice of turning Prospero into Prospera. This necessitated a little bit of rewriting of the backstory, achieved by means of some invented lines that imitate Shakespearean language and rhythms quite as effectively as Dryden and Davenant did in their reworking for *The Enchanted Island*. Even people who know the original text well will struggle to pick out exactly which lines are the invented ones in the retrospective narrative early in the movie.

The effect of turning Prospero the father into Prospera the mother is striking. Some modern critics detect a disturbing sexual possessiveness in Prospero's admonitions about Ferdinand and Miranda not sleeping together before they are married. Shakespeare's main purpose was to stress the importance of legitimacy and respect in the marital union, not least because it is the basis for a political union of Milan and Naples. With Taymor's gender reassignment, Prospera's solicitude for Miranda becomes maternal in a wholly natural way. The somewhat anachronistic quasi-Freudian reading of father and daughter is stripped away. Mirren's Prospera can be irascible and forceful, but she becomes truly herself when she is being tender—with Miranda, with Ariel, and even (in certain looks of pity and wonder) with Caliban.

The casting as Caliban of Djimon Hounsou, born in Benin, West Africa, might suggest that this movie will offer a reading of *The Tempest* that emphasizes racial oppression and colonial dispossession. The play was written at the dawn of the British Empire. It draws on information about the Virginia settlement and the shipwreck, near Bermuda, of the colonial governor. The dynamic of Caliban's enslavement and the ironic reference to a "brave new world" has made *The Tempest* a key text in the story of empire and subsequently of postcolonialism. One of the great apostles of colonial liberation, Frantz Fanon, wrote his foundational anti-imperialist political treatise *Prospero and Caliban: Black Skin, White Masks* as a response to a book by Octave Mannoni called *The Psychology of Colonization*, which argued that Prospero was the archetype of the colonizer, Caliban of the colonized.

Some viewers may make these connections, but Taymor has absolutely resisted the temptation to foreground them in a polemical or didactic way. She is too interested in the dynamics of the relationships between the characters, in the poetry and its supporting music, in the colors and textures of the environment, above all in the transformational magic of art itself, to be distracted by "politically correct" reading.

Where Hounsou's African inheritance genuinely is relevant is in the area of magic. In Benin, witchcraft is still real. In the movement of his body, the play of his words, the darkness of his imagined fears, he taps into a dimension that cannot be contained by the constraints of western rationalism.

And this becomes another respect in which the feminization of Prospero into Prospera becomes inspired. Caliban is the son of Sycorax, who is accused of witchcraft. Prospera recognizes a resemblance between her own dark arts and those of Sycorax. They both have power to bedim the noonday sun, to raise a storm, even to open graves and make the dead walk. The more Prospera protests that her magic is white whereas that of Sycorax was black, the less convinced we become that black and white magic can be kept neatly apart in separate boxes.

Shakespeare knew this and subtly intimated it to his more educated audience members. When he came to write the great speech in which Prospero abjures "this rough magic," Shakespeare went back to the book in which he had learned about magic, about those ancient stories we call "myths," about poetry, about transformation, about strong passions, about the symbiosis of humankind and nature: Ovid's *Metamorphoses*. He turned to the incantation of the witch Medea. "Ye elves of hills, brooks, standing lakes and groves" is a direct quotation from Ovid's "auraeque et venti montesque amnesque lacusque, / dique omnes nemorum, dique omnes noctis adeste" (assisted by Arthur Golding's English translation of Ovid, which Shakespeare must have had open on his desk as he wrote: "Ye airs and winds: ye elves of hills, of brooks, of woods alone, / Of standing lakes, and of the night, approach ye everyone").

That the black arts of the *female* witch Medea are the source for Prospero's seemingly white magic is justification in itself for the switch to Prospera and the casting of Mirren. But the connection also reminds us of the complexity of the Shakespearean vision, the difficulty of assuming easy distinctions between good and evil in the world of his plays. Like Ovid, Shakespeare is interested in the mingled yarn of our human fabric. Both are writers who probe our humanity with great rigor, but ultimately they do so in a spirit of sympathy for our frailties and indulgences, rather than stern judgment upon our faults.

And with a great deal of comedy along the way: Shakespeare had the best comedians of his age at his command, so he nearly always made sure there was a role for the company clown. One of the incidental triumphs of Taymor's movie is that she has found in Russell Brand a true successor to Robert Armin, the master of witty and irreverent words for whom Shakespeare wrote the delicious part of Trinculo.

When Shakespeare wrote *The Tempest*, he was able to call on a rich mix of old and new talent. Richard Burbage, who had taken the lead in all the great tragedies, would have been Prospero. The wise old counselor Gonzalo may well have been Hemmings, another trusted colleague who had been there from the start of Shakespeare's career. Several of the former apprentices who had played female parts while in their teens had by now graduated to become full members of the company. The part of Caliban may well have been written with one of them in mind. And there was a new generation of boy players in training. Two of them would have risen to the challenge of playing Miranda and Ariel.

So too with Taymor's casting. Having long since played Cleopatra, Lady Macbeth, and Ophelia for the Royal Shakespeare Company, Helen Mirren has the rhythms of Shakespearean verse in her blood. Tom Conti, who plays Gonzalo, is one of Britain's most seasoned character actors. Alan Cumming, who did brilliant work for Taymor as

the villainous Saturninus in *Titus*, brings animation to the difficult role of cynical Sebastian. Chris Cooper and David Strathairn capture the sharp difference between the sullenly unrepentant Antonio and the penitent Alonso. The versatile Alfred Molina makes Stephano very funny, but also tender. As for the new generation, Felicity Jones and Reeve Carney capture all the freshness and wonder of Miranda and Ferdinand's young love, while Ben Whishaw's Ariel is a performance of astonishing emotional range delivered with quickness of motion and ravishing beauty of voice in both speech and song.

Music, so essential to Shakespeare's Blackfriars style, is at the heart of the movie, as it was in Taymor's original stage production. It is fitting that *The Tempest* draws on the proto-operatic genre of the masque and that in its later stage history the play was converted into an opera, since this is the play in which Shakespeare was reaching toward what Richard Wagner would one day call the *Gesamtkunstwerk*, the total work of art, the integration of poetry, music, and stage-design. In the two centuries between Davenant and Wagner, opera was the total art form, but in the twentieth and twenty-first centuries its place has been taken by film.

The closing credit roll of Julie Taymor's *Tempest* is perhaps the most beautiful such sequence of film ever made. No other medium could so ravishingly bring together the poetry of Shakespeare's epilogue, a hauntingly sung musical setting, and the visual image of Prospera's drowned books. In the hands of a master director at the height of her magical powers, this is a total work of art.

R O U G H   M A G I C /

Julie Taymor

DRIVEN BY THE BITTERNESS AND FURY OF ITS LEAD CHARACTER, the sorceress/ scientist Prospera, *The Tempest* is at once a revenge drama, a romance, and a black comedy. It is the mother's protective love for her daughter, Miranda, that fuels the tempest she has conjured and all the subsequent events on the island in the space of a day. . . .

Shakespeare was the ultimate screenwriter. More of his plays have been made into movies than any other writer's. His palette was immense, limited only by the boundaries of his imagination. In *The Tempest* he wrote of real and fantasy worlds, philosophies, both lofty and poetical, juxtaposed with rock-bottom crude and scatological fare. Young lovers in the mode of Romeo and Juliet are scripted with an understanding of the delicate, vulnerable, and awkward comedy that comes with first love. Smashed up against these scenes stumble the abominations of three of Shakespeare's best and bawdiest lowlifes. And mirroring this comic trio's treacherous escapades are the wicked, cynical, and corrupt lords, whose lives get turned upside down in the maelstrom of Prospera's unrelenting vengeance. In addition to the human characters, Shakespeare created a most singular and complex being in the form of the spirit Ariel.

The Tempest, in other words, offers a great opportunity for a film director—from its wondrous and diverse parts for actors to visual dimensions and challenges that are ripe to be realized through extraordinary locations and experimental visual effects.

The first Shakespeare that I directed in the theater was *The Tempest*, on a small stage in New York City in 1986. The play began with the silhouette of a young girl building a sandcastle on the top of a black sandhill. Suddenly a stagehand, garbed in black and holding a large watering can, ran to the young girl and started to pour water onto the castle. As the lights shifted focus, illuminating only the castle and the falling water, this mundane image was transformed into a "rainstorm" that dissolved the fragile castle into the earth. Though Prospero's "magic" was exposed through the art of theater lighting, the audience was invited to believe that the tempest had begun. In this moment the theatrical conventions, the rules of the production, were laid out. The form and style of theatrical storytelling illuminated the substantive meaning of the piece—Prospero was the ultimate puppet master, the engineer and string-puller of illusions.

The crew helps Prospera's robe move in the wind

REVEALING THE MECHANICS of the theater creates its own alchemy, its rough magic, and the audience willingly plays "make-believe." In cinema, however, where one can actually film on real locations and create seemingly naturalistic events, the temptation is to throw away the artifice and go for the literal reality. There is something inherently sad about this. Even in fantasy cinema the audience expects the worlds that are created to feel "real," or at least plausible, and it is not required of viewers that they fill in the blanks or suspend their disbelief.

In the film of *The Tempest* I had an opportunity to act on these two impulses: to combine the literal reality of location—its natural light, winds, and rough seas—with conjured visual effects that subvert the "natural" and toy with it. As in the theater version, we begin the film with the close-up image of a black sandcastle. The camera pulls away, and we realize that the castle is tiny, fitting onto the palm of a hand. Rain begins to fall and the castle dissolves through fingers as the camera finally reveals the surprised expression of the young girl belonging to the hand, Miranda. Lightning cracks, and we cut to what she sees: the wide roiling sea and a distant ship caught in a ferocious storm. The long shot of the tempest looks like a Turner painting come to life. The juxtaposition of these two moments and the play with perception and scale signals the style of the film: from visceral reality to heightened expressionism.

At the start of the drama, one of the major themes of the play is posited: Nature versus Nurture. In one brief ideograph, civilization, represented by the simple form of a child's sandcastle, is destroyed in a downpour. The perilous storm that destroys the ship also establishes this theme, by exposing the fact that the lofty position of the king onboard is rendered meaningless when Nature is in control. The irony is that it is Prospera who, at this moment in time, is in control of Nature. Her conflict with the abuse and renunciation of such power unfolds as another critical theme of *The Tempest*.

THE PLAYERS

I have chosen to discuss three of the main characters in these notes, as they proved to be the most conceptually challenging. The decision to switch the gender of the lead character, renamed Prospera, was a diving board to a whole new appreciation of the play. Shakespeare's unique creations, Ariel and Caliban, are ripe for endless interpretations. Emblematic and surreal, they require total invention in shaping and designing the presentation of their natures. In terms of alchemical symbolism, Prospera's two "servants" represent opposites, the earth and the air, within and without, that she struggles to unite and ultimately release.

Taymor directing Helen Mirren

PROSPERA

Having twice directed the play with "Prospero" as the principal character, I made subtle discoveries with the gender change to "Prospera." The reason I decided to make the switch had everything to do with Helen Mirren and a coincidental exchange that we had while I was mulling over possible actors for the part. Once I fixated on her for the role, examination of the text and how it would change became illuminating. Except for the obvious "he's" to "she's" and "sir" to "mum" or "ma'am," very little would need to be altered to accommodate the change.

The major adjustment to the text was in the reshaping of the character's backstory, which I reconceived, and which my colleague, Glen Berger, put into verse. In this version, Prospera becomes the widow and heir to the deceased Duke of Milan. Like the original Prospero, she has studied the alchemical arts, though, in her case, it has been in secret, as women were often forbidden this path of study. Once Prospera inherits her dukedom, Antonio, her ambitious and treacherous brother, accuses her of witchcraft, punishable by death at the stake. Here we resume the original text, which describes how the faithful councilor, Gonzalo, helps to save Prospera and her four-year-old daughter, Miranda, by secreting them aboard a small bark and sending them out to sea. Their survival is a miracle.

When we first meet Prospera, she has already suffered twelve years of exile. As sole ruler on an almost deserted island, she is at once

Taymor setting up a shot

study of nature in order to understand and control its positive forces. Given that Nature is identified as "The Mother," knowledge of the medicinal elements of the earth has traditionally been the purview of women. The battle, however, between white and black magic begins in our story on the island, with the enslavement of Caliban. It is brought into sharp focus as Prospera spews her disdain for the "foul witch, Sycorax," the mother of Caliban and torturer of Ariel. At the top of the story, Prospera does not yet recognize or acknowledge her own dark side, but as the play progresses Prospera and Sycorax become mirrors to one another in their malignant and abusive use of the black arts.

Helen Mirren brings many conflicting impulses to her Prospera, which makes her a classic protagonist in Shakespeare's canon. With her erratic fury, cruelty, maternal warmth, cold authority, and poetic introspection, she plays the witch, the scientist, the poet, the ferocious tiger protecting her cub, the steely leader, and more. It is not neat. She is not perfect or benign, but twisted by a tempest within that stems from guilt over her daughter's innocent exile and the urgency to exact revenge on those responsible.

To Miranda, in explaining the tempest she has conjured:

PROSPERA
I have done nothing but in care of thee,
Of thee, my dear one, thee, my daughter, who
Art ignorant of what thou art, nought knowing
Of whence I am, nor that I am more better
Than Prospera, master of a full poor cell,
And thy no greater mother.

And later, concerning her enemies . . .

I will plague them all, even to roaring!

ARIEL
Ariel is the embodiment in spirit of human emotion, vulnerability, and compassion. How does an actor play pure spirit, both and beyond male and female, appearing and disappearing on command, able to change shape and size, and yet able to move the audience to laughter or tears? In the theater I utilized the art of puppetry in the form of a disembodied mask that could be moved in any direction, defying gravity and human limitations. The purely theatrical choice was quite moving precisely because the artifice was so blatant, yet could project subtle emotions. In the film, however, the character of Ariel was conceived as an actor's fully human performance treated with the use of cinematic visual effects. The challenge was to retain the visceral, nuanced performance that only a human can give, while transforming

the master despot and the vengeful mother. Her source of power stems from a mother's natural and ferocious protective passion and a scholar/scientist's obsession with the ability to control nature for both dark and benign purposes.

The themes of power, revenge, compassion, and forgiveness become more complex in the relationships that Prospera has with Miranda, Ferdinand (Miranda's lover), Ariel, and Caliban. Prospera's protective feelings for her daughter are quite different than those of a father. There is no male rivalry with the young suitor; no "honor defiled" in the attempted rape scenario by Caliban. Instead, Prospera's actions are a direct result of her knowing intimately what Miranda is experiencing as a young virginal woman and where the dangers lie. In this gender twist, it is partly because Prospera is a woman that her dukedom could be stolen from her, and the bitterness of this fact infiltrates and heightens the tension of all of her interactions with the other characters on the island.

These are subtle nuances that in no way alter the essence of Shakespeare's play, but rather give it another layer of depth and a new way to experience a familiar tale. In doing research on the play I was surprised to discover that the well-known speech of Prospera's that begins "Ye elves of hills, standing lakes and groves" is almost identical to the witch Medea's speech in Ovid's *Metamorphoses*. The identification and accusation of Prospera as a witch begins in the Milan flashback. Yet she sees herself as an alchemist, a scientist, engaged in the

Taymor directing Djimon Hounsou in Lanai's Garden of the Gods

his physical presence into essences of light, fire, wind, and water, and the corporeal manifestation of harpies, frogs, stinging bees, and bubbling lava.

In casting Ben Whishaw, I had to accept a significant condition: he would be unavailable until the end of the shoot and thus never on location with us in Hawaii. That meant that Helen would have to film most of her Ariel scenes without Ariel. It was a daunting, yet fortuitous challenge. After all, Ariel is not human, does not walk on the ground, and is constantly transforming. This limitation was an invitation to Kyle Cooper, the visual effects designer, and myself to invent an entirely new way of combining a live actor's performance with CGI. Because of Ben's availability, most of his performance was filmed in the studio, in front of a green screen, making it possible for us to manipulate his image in postproduction and place him in the preshot backgrounds with Helen.

Not all of his scenes were shot this way, however. It was important for some of their most intense exchanges that Helen and Ben be able to act together. We were then left to alter his arrivals and exits, his physical form, whether it be translucent, grossly deformed, or multiplied, with the help of postproduction effects. A few scenes, such as his appearance as a sea nymph with Ferdinand, were shot through a large glass frame containing a few inches of water. Ben was underneath, able to move freely and speak his lines, yet his image appears to be fractured and distorted through the lens of water— the miracle is that the effect is live, in camera, and not computer generated. It was extremely liberating to be able to preserve a great actor's performance and yet transform him into the various elements and creatures that are delineated by the text.

There is one scene, however, in which I purposefully left Ariel untreated, corporeal. It is an intimate scene with Prospera in her cell. Her enemies have been brought low and she asks Ariel how they are faring.

ARIEL
. . . Your charm so strongly works 'em
That if you now beheld them, your affections
Would become tender.

PROSPERA
Dost thou think so, spirit?

ARIEL
Mine would, master, were I human.

Because this is the first time that we see the fully human being of Ariel, every little nuance of expression becomes that much more intense and felt. This is the scene that finally leads Prospera to understand that "the rarer action is in virtue than in vengeance." And it is the spirit, Ariel, as an agent of reconciliation, who signifies this compassion, forgiveness, and ultimate redemption.

CALIBAN
He is described as "thou earth thou," a foul-smelling "plain fish," "puppy-headed monster," a "poisonous slave," the bastard of an evil witch, and guilty of the near rape of Miranda, Prospera's precious daughter. Caliban may also be perceived as simply a native of this remote island, and the above depictions a product of the prejudicial point of view of the Europeans who are shipwrecked on it, in particular those of Prospera, who now governs the island and Caliban as her own. In casting an African in this role, one automatically brings to the forefront the obvious themes of colonialization and usurpation that clearly were part of Shakespeare's worldview, derived from stories culled from explorations to Africa and the New World.

But in order to truly serve Shakespeare's unique vision of this character, one must go beyond sociopolitical commentary achieved through a casting choice. Djimon Hounsou went through a four-hour makeup ordeal every day to achieve the look of his Caliban. His skin was made to resemble the island's cracked red earth and black lava rock, with raised scars of obscenities he had carved into his flesh.

CALIBAN
You taught me language, and my profit on't

The crew shooting Alan Cumming

Mark Friedberg, the production designer, with Taymor   Sandy Powell, the costume designer   Françoise Bonnot, the editor, with Taymor

Is, I know how to curse. The red plague rid you
For learning me your language!

The nickname "Mooncalf," endearingly coined by Stephano for Caliban, suggested the white circular moon that frames his one blue eye, which in itself was motivated by the notion that he is the whelp of that "blue-eyed hag," Sycorax. The "calf" part of the equation is delivered in the maplike patches of white on black skin that add to the "otherness" of this unique racial mash-up. The webbing between his fingers adds that touch of monster fantasy that speaks to the "strange fish," as Trinculo calls him. All in all, this Caliban, both beautiful and grotesque, is the island; Nature personified. And Djimon's athletic and antic movement, inspired by the Japanese dance form Butoh, completes his physical embodiment.

In casting Djimon Hounsou in this role we were privileged to have not only a great actor but one who brought with him experience, belief, and respect for the power of white and black magic. His personal stories of sorcery in his country, Benin, were both inspiring and harrowing. There was never any question in Djimon's mind that the figure Helen was playing, the sorceress, could control Caliban. He is the "natural" that Prospera tries and fails to reform in her nurturing. Their clashes leave the audience discomforted, unsure as to whom to root for, as Shakespeare never chooses sides. Djimon's Caliban is multifaceted: he can be physically threatening and violent in one scene and naïve and puppylike in another. He is comedic, foolish, elementally human, and profoundly tragic, bestowed with the innate intelligence to speak some of the most elegant and moving poetry of *The Tempest*.

PRODUCTION DESIGN

THE ISLAND

In choosing the location for the film, I decided to go for an existing island rather than create a wholly fabricated and theatrical environment. The islands of Lanai and the Big Island of Hawaii offered us the perfect landscapes to shoot all of the exterior scenes: black volcanic rock, red earth canyons, white coral bones, and a deep blue sea. The alchemist's sandbox—a tabula rasa for Prospera's powers.

As in my film *Titus*, location is metaphor and represents the essence of a scene in a visual ideograph. I took as a cue a line of Caliban's to Prospera, in their first scene together: "and here you sty me in this hard rock, whiles you do keep from me the rest o' th' island." Caliban's emergence out of the harsh, barren landscape of lava rock supports Shakespeare's verbal imagery. The volcanic terrain of the two islands was the draw, with not a palm tree in sight. Not only did these infinite, black jagged fields feel surreal and highly theatrical, but they represented the inner landscapes of the characters inhabiting

Stuart Dryburgh, the director of photography, with Taymor

Kyle Cooper, the visual effects supervisor

them. The stark minimalism highlighted emotional states without unnecessary distractions and details.

Among other locations on Lanai was a gnarled, brambled fairy-tale forest, which fit the thorny, drunken squabbles of the clowns, while labyrinthine ironwoods worked to disorient the court and set the stage for conspiracy. A deep red-sand canyon lit by golden sunlight served to put the two lovers in each other's laps and created the sensual setting for their inevitable fall into love. And of course there was always the surrounding sea, a constant reminder of the isolation of the island and the power of the ever-changing natural elements.

THE CELL

Although Mark Friedberg, our production designer, was instrumental in pinning down locations on the islands, his real magic was in his design of the sets that were used at the end of the shoot. In Steiner Studios in Brooklyn, he built Prospera's cell and inner courtyard. Relying heavily on the colors of the islands, the cell's white coral walls, red earth floor, and black lava pool comprised an alchemical, geometric design that transcended a specific time period. Its two giant walls stood at right angles, like an open book, once again following the premise that location is metaphor. At the top of the frozen lava-raked floor was a small library, which held Prospera's books in its carved igneous rock walls. The garden exhibited her botanical creations with wild hybrids of

fruit trees, flowers, and medicinal plants. The half-moon pool was a practical cistern, but functioned also as a sacred space, a black womb from which Prospera could conjure the benevolent spirit Ariel or demonic lava dogs, as the pure water transformed into bubbling molten lava.

Once we chose to shoot on a real island, we needed to see how Prospera and Miranda lived and survived on the island during those twelve years. The inner cell off the courtyard appeared to be a natural underground cave that mirrored the cliff walls on Lanai. In contrast to the starkness of the exterior locations, this human habitation was filled with objects of culture: books, specimens, a loom, fabrics, utensils, and oil lamps—the "nurture" elements retained from civilization. The wreck of the small bark that brought them to the island now functioned as their bed. Most of the cave was devoted to Prospera's alchemical laboratory, with handblown vials containing herbs, oils, and serums. In the center of the room was an open fire furnace with a large bellows, harnessing the underground energy of the volcano.

In shooting, the controllable intimacy of the cave offered a respite from the exterior scenes that were subject to the tyranny of the elements and the limitations of daylight. While outdoors, we utilized a "day for night" technique in camera to give a surreal flavor to the solar-eclipse sequences. In the studio, however, Stuart Dryburgh, our director of photography, was able to design and control the lighting to maximum effect.

Composer Elliot Goldenthal   Lynn Hendee, producer   Robert Chartoff, producer

COSTUMES

As the island and Prospera's cell do not suggest a specific time period, the only clue to when our drama takes place would be in the costumes. Sandy Powell, the costume designer, and I wanted to play with time by mixing elements of period costumes according to the nature of the characters. We wanted to connect to historical moments and styles while also feeling quite contemporary.

In essence Prospera herself is a volcano, burning from within, primed to erupt and destroy, but ultimately to redeem and regenerate. Sandy and I discussed using the image of the volcano for Prospera's two main costumes on the island. Her magic robe is made of shards of blue/black volcanic rock placed in diagonal flows on a large conical shape. It is more a sculpture than a robe. Her everyday tunic is of natural indigo-dyed fabric, stitched together in layers, also like lava flow.

Her staff is made from black obsidian rock, which possesses an innate magical power to those cultures that live on volcanic terrain. As Prospera is both mother and father to Miranda and master on the island, her dress and hair are practical, masculine and feminine. She stands out of time and specific cultural reference. However, in the flashback scenes to Milan, Prospera wears dark European clothing that evokes the paintings of Velázquez, with a modern twist of zippers instead of lace. Her severe female dress is tightly corseted, and the ruff that chokes her neck is the closest sign that hearkens to the sixteenth century, the age of conquistadors.

Once Prospera's mission is accomplished, her enemies punished, and her magic abjured, she asks Ariel to deliver to her the garments she once wore in Milan. As he laces her corset tightly, her face reveals the sacrifice that she is making. As a woman, the power and the freedom she has wielded on the island will now be subject to the rules of the society to which she returns. Of course, in the traditional reading of the play where Prospero is dressed in his Duke's robe and hat, the event represents quite the opposite meaning; his authority and status are still intact.

Miranda, in her homespun off-white shift, is garbed like her mother, in practical clothing for the island and for all time. Only when she is formally betrothed to Ferdinand does she don a formfitting corset that presages her return to courtly European life and her rigid status within that world.

The shipwrecked Italian court—King Alonso, Prince Ferdinand, Gonzalo, Antonio, and Sebastian—are dressed in the same formal manner as Prospera is for Milan. Their black, metallic, and severe silhouettes are in utter contrast to the organic colors and forms of nature that confront them. Though they feel the most "period," their costumes too make use of twentieth-century flourishes, with jodhpurs, military boots, and zipper details.

The "clowns," Stephano and Trinculo, wear the only bright colors, with costumes of lime greens and wine reds in stripes and plaids that add a bit of zaniness to the ensemble. Even though the period of their costumes is a complete patchwork of time, we wanted a Dickensian feel. The court jester, Trinculo, with his sewer-rat false teeth and wormy long hair, slinks through the landscape in an exaggerated tailcoat and pointy shoes. A crew-cutted Stephano, the drunken butler, eventually strips down to a filthy singlet that barely covers his paunch. These two comic lowlifes would slit your throat while they make you laugh.

Ariel and Caliban do not wear costumes. Their naked forms required a makeup design that helped to define the essence of their character, or characters, as in the case of Ariel.

MUSIC

In composing the score for *The Tempest*, Elliot Goldenthal, our composer, was faced with three challenges. The first was to find an overall sonority for the island setting, in which fantastical and psychological forces are locked in a dance of retribution and forgiveness. The grand plan was to use amplified guitars in various ranges and alternative tunings, along with a symphonic string orchestra to create a sense of timeless presentness. With this sonic palette, he could then meet the second challenge, which was to paint more specific distinctions between the individual sets of characters by using additional instrumental colors, such as glass armonica and non-western flutes for Ariel, steel cello for the somber sorrows of the court or Prospera's introspective moments, and a wide range of percussion and didgeridoo for Caliban and his coconspirators. The third challenge was to set a number of on-camera songs (that Shakespeare indicated in the play) for Stephano, Caliban, and Ariel as well as two additional non-indicated songs, one for Ferdinand and another for Prospera's final speech.

PROSPERA'S CODA

Now my charms are all o'erthrown,
And what strength I have's mine own,
Which is most faint.
Oh release me from my bands
With the help of your good hands.
Gentle breath of yours my sails
Must fill, or else my project fails,
Which was to please. Now I lack
Spirits to enforce, art to enchant,
And my ending is despair,
Unless I be relieved by prayer,
Which pierces so that it assaults
Mercy itself and frees all faults.
As you from crimes would pardon'd be,
Let your indulgence set me free.

The "Coda" is one of Shakespeare's most famous speeches, as it is widely believed to represent his farewell to the world as an artist. Normally in theater performances it is delivered with the houselights on, all artifice removed, and is directed to the audience. I had originally cut it from the filmscript because I felt that Prospera speaking directly to the camera for this last moment of the film was one speech too many and in no way could equal the effect it has in the live theater. The film's last image of Prospera on the ocean cliff, her back to the camera, tossing her magic staff to the dark rocks below, and the staff's subsequent shattering, is the ending. But when all was cut and timed and scored and mixed, the rhythm of the end of the film felt truncated, incomplete. I asked Elliot to take those last great words and set them to music for the seven-minute-long end-title sequence. And to that haunting female vocal, sung by Beth Gibbons, the credits rolled and we drowned the books of Prospera in the deep dark sea.

CAST

PROSPERA Helen Mirren

ARIEL Ben Whishaw

CALIBAN Djimon Hounsou

ANTONIO Chris Cooper

SEBASTIAN Alan Cumming

GONZALO Tom Conti

MIRANDA Felicity Jones   FERDINAND Reeve Carney   BOATSWAIN Jude Akuwidike

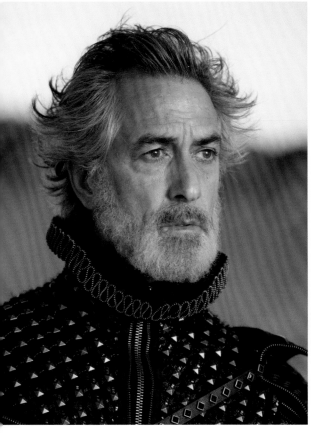

ALONSO David Strathairn   TRINCULO Russell Brand   STEPHANO Alfred Molina

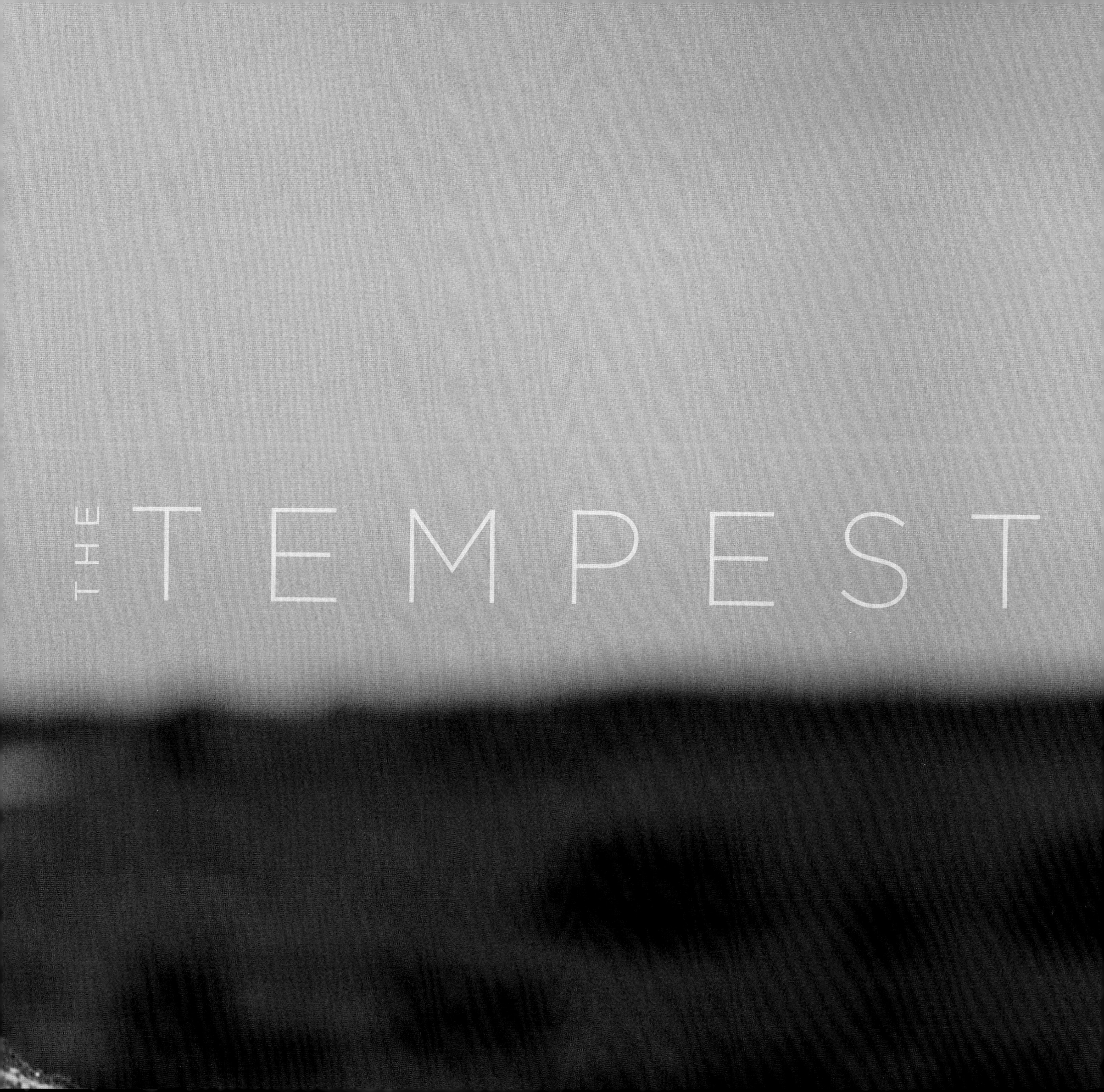
THE TEMPEST

EXT. BLACK SAND BEACH - DAY

An intricate black sand castle with medieval turrets and walls is set against a clear blue sky.

Ominous, dark clouds form in the background. Large drops of rain begin to fall on the castle, and it commences to disintegrate.

As the camera pulls away from the sand castle, we reveal that it is a miniature sitting in the palm of MIRANDA'S hand.

MIRANDA, a wild, natural beauty and tomboy of sixteen years, looks dismayed as the castle dissolves into mud and drips through her fingers.

As the pelting rain beats down on her face, MIRANDA'S eyes dart to the open sea, where she spies a sailing ship caught in the midst of the tempest.

EXT. SHIP AT SEA - STORM - DAY

The KING'S ship is enveloped by a full-scale storm—thunder, lightning, and mammoth swells crashing over the decks.

The SHIPMASTER, BOATSWAIN, and MARINERS try in vain to sail the ship as fire ignites the sails and the main mast splinters.

The action will intercut between the top deck, the crow's nest, and the cabins below. We are on the ship.

A rough and weathered BOATSWAIN shouts orders to the sailors through the howling winds.

> BOATSWAIN
> Yare, yare! Take in the topsail.
> Tend to the master's whistle!
> Fall to't yarely, or we run ourselves aground.
> Bestir, bestir!

ALONSO, the KING, a powerful presence brought low with the fear of disaster, emerges from his cabin.

He is followed by his young son, Prince FERDINAND, and GONZALO, his faithful old counselor.

> ALONSO
> Good Boatswain, have care. Where's the master?
> Play the men.

> BOATSWAIN
> I pray now, keep below.

> ALONSO
> (annoyed)
> Where is the master, bos'n?

With a sarcastic nod to the angry sky the BOATSWAIN blasts the KING.

> BOATSWAIN
> Do you not hear him?
> You mar our labor, keep your cabins: you do assist the storm.

Shocked by the insolence of the BOATSWAIN, the good old counselor intervenes.

> GONZALO
> Nay, good, be patient.

> BOATSWAIN
> When the sea is. Hence! What cares these roarers
> for the name of king? To cabin! Silence!
> Trouble us not.

ANTONIO, the conniving Duke of Milan, and SEBASTIAN, the oily and petrified younger brother of the KING, have been watching this interaction.

Fearful for their lives they hasten below.

> GONZALO
> Good, yet remember whom thou hast aboard.

> BOATSWAIN
> None that I more love than myself.
> You are a counselor; if you can command
> these elements to silence, and work the
> peace of the present, we will not hand
> a rope more. Use your authority.

Unable to respond to the challenge, GONZALO and the KING stand paralyzed.

FERDINAND, in an attempt to defend his father's honor and position, moves to admonish the impertinent BOATSWAIN but is pushed aside.

> BOATSWAIN (CONT'D)
> Out of our way, I say!

GONZALO tries to comfort the furious but diminished KING as they make their way below.

> GONZALO
> I have great comfort from this fellow.
> Methinks he hath no drowning mark upon him.

EXT. ROCKY SHORELINE - DAY

MIRANDA, traversing the black coral flats, runs through the storm in the direction of the high cliffs.

Her bare feet nimbly fly over the rocky terrain.

INT. KING'S CABIN - DAY

The storm in full throttle.

GONZALO bursts open the door to find KING ALONSO and his son on their knees, desperately at prayers, as the furniture tumbles and slides across the room.

> BOATSWAIN (O.C.)
> Down with the topmast! Yare! Lower, lower!
> Bring her to try with main-course.

EXT. TOP DECK - DAY

SEBASTIAN and ANTONIO return to the top deck to the annoyance of the beleaguered BOATSWAIN.

BOATSWAIN
Yet again? What do you here? Shall we give o'er,
And drown? Have you a mind to sink?

SEBASTIAN
A pox o' your throat, you bawling, blasphemous,
Incharitable dog!

BOATSWAIN
Work you, then.

ANTONIO
Hang, cur, hang! You whoreson, insolent noisemaker,
We are less afraid to be drowned than thou art.

BOATSWAIN
Lay her a-hold, a-hold! Set her two courses! Off to sea again!
Lay her off!

MARINERS
All lost! To prayers, to prayers! All lost!

BOATSWAIN
What, must our mouths be cold?

The MARINERS slide off the deck into the sea, as the water engulfs the flaming, sinking ship.

MARINER #1
Mercy on us!

MARINER #2
We split, we split!

MARINER #3
Farewell, my wife and children!

MARINER #1
Farewell, brother!

MARINERS
We split, we split, we split!

Hell is empty and all the devils here!

INT. KING'S CABIN - DAY

FERDINAND kneels before the large flaming cross, which crashes to the floor, catching fire to all it touches.

> FERDINAND
> Hell is empty and all the devils here!

An explosion of water bursts through the cabin window, swallowing the room.

EXT. CLIFF PROMONTORY - DAY

The storm still rages as PROSPERA leans into the wild wind, her face a mirror of the tempest.

With grim determination she holds her obsidian staff stretched out before her in the direction of the burning, sinking ship.

Her magical robe, composed of shards of glass and light, whips about her.

EXT. STEEP PATH UP THE CLIFF - DAY

MIRANDA scrambles up the path in the still-pelting rain.

EXT. CLIFF PROMONTORY - DAY

She falls to her knees, hanging onto her mother as the storm begins to subside.

> MIRANDA
>> If by your art, my dearest mother, you have
>> Put the wild waters in this roar, allay them.
>>> O, I have suffered
>> With those that I saw suffer. A brave vessel,
>> Who had, no doubt, some noble creature in her,
>> Dash'd all to pieces.
>>> Poor souls, they perish'd!

Through the tears and drops of rain that stream down her face, MIRANDA flashes a defiant face up toward her mother.

With one flourish of her staff, PROSPERA causes the storm to subside.

Slowly she comes out of her trance.

> PROSPERA
>> Be collected.
>> No more amazement: tell your piteous heart
>> There's no harm done.

MIRANDA rushes to the cliff's edge, searching for any sign of the ship.

> MIRANDA
>> O, woe the day!

> PROSPERA
>> No harm.

MIRANDA turns to her mother, shaken and bewildered.

PROSPERA takes her daughter into her arms, holding her firmly.

> PROSPERA (CONT'D)
>> I have done nothing but in care of thee,
>> Of thee, my dear one, thee, my daughter, who
>> Art ignorant of what thou art, nought knowing
>> Of whence I am, nor that I am more better
>> Than Prospera, master of a full poor cell,
>> And thy no greater mother.

> MIRANDA
>> More to know
>> Did never meddle with my thoughts.

> PROSPERA
>> 'Tis time
>> I should inform thee farther.

INT. PROSPERA'S CELL - DAY

The cell is an underground cave, lit by daylight that streams through cracks in the stone ceiling then bounces throughout the chambers via reflectors made of mirror stone.

In the darker recesses, the cave is illuminated by fire from glass bowls of palm oil.

At one end of the cell is a room with a natural furnace of fire burning brightly and kept alive by a bellows contraption connected to bamboo pipes conducting wind from a mill above ground.

The fire is from the volcanic lava flowing deep within the earth's core.

Handblown glass vials filled with various liquids, seeds, and strange plants sit on rough-hewn tables: a homemade alchemist's laboratory.

In other parts of the cell are signs of domestic life: a primitive loom and spinning wheel, a bed constructed from a portion of a small, wrecked boat, books, etc.

The flickering light casts shadows on the walls of the cave.

PROSPERA carefully hangs her magic robe before a special "altar."

> PROSPERA
> So.
> Lie there, my art.

MIRANDA, wrapped in a blanket, warms herself before the fire.

> **PROSPERA (CONT'D)**
> Wipe thou thine eyes; have comfort.
> The direful spectacle of the wreck, which touch'd
> The very virtue of compassion in thee,
> I have with such provision in mine art
> So safely ordered that there is no soul—

MIRANDA starts to question her mother but is stopped.

> **PROSPERA (CONT'D)**
> No, not so much perdition as an hair
> Betid to any creature in the vessel
> Which thou heard'st cry, which thou saw'st sink.
> Sit down, and be attentive. Canst thou remember
> A time before we came unto this cell?
> I do not think thou canst, for then thou wast not
> Out three years old.

> **MIRANDA**
> Certainly, ma'am, I can.

> **PROSPERA**
> By what? By any other house or person?
> Of any thing the image tell me that
> Hath kept with thy remembrance.

> **MIRANDA**
> 'Tis far off, and rather like a dream.
> Had I not
> Four or five women once that tended me?

> **PROSPERA**
> Thou hadst, and more, Miranda.
> Twelve year since, Miranda, twelve year since,
> Thy mother held the Dukedom of Milan
> And its princely power.

> **MIRANDA**
> But are not you my mother?

> **PROSPERA**
> The very same, who long ago was wife
> To him who ruled Milan most liberally;

Who, with as tolerant a hand toward me,
Gave license to my long hours in pursuit
Of hidden truths, of coiled powers contained
Within some elements to harm, or heal.
I brooked no interruption but your squalling;
For thou, child, art a princess born.

MIRANDA
O heavens!
What foul play had we, that we came from thence?

INT./EXT. CAVE CELL INTERCUT WITH SCENES IN MILAN

As PROSPERA tells their story to MIRANDA, we flash back, in quick fragments, to various images in Milan:

PROSPERA works intently in her LIBRARY/LABORATORY as her husband lovingly watches her from the doorway. A cradle lies at her feet, the infant, MIRANDA, crying.

In a CHAPEL, at the funeral of her HUSBAND, the Duke, a royal crowd assembles

in prayer. ANTONIO, PROSPERA'S brother, looks to his sister with concern.

At a meeting in the STATE ROOM with her counselors, PROSPERA, the new Duke, signs documents as her brother looks on with envy.

In the castle shadows, ANTONIO conspires with the KING, while SEBASTIAN looks on.

The KING'S MEN break into PROSPERA'S alchemical LAB and smash all of her instruments.

In the dead of night, PROSPERA and the now four-year-old MIRANDA are violently torn out of bed by armored guards.

While the city sleeps, PROSPERA and her YOUNG DAUGHTER are secreted into a BOAT by old GONZALO and sent off to sea.

PROSPERA
Upon thy father's death, authority was
Conferred (as was his will) to me alone,
Thereby awaking the ambitions of
My brother and thy uncle, call'd Antonio—
Thou attendst not—

MIRANDA
Good Madam, I do!

PROSPERA
I pray thee, mark me—that a brother should
Be so perfidious!—he whom I did charge
To execute express commands as to
The prudent governing of fair Milan,
Instead undid, subverted— Dost thou attend me?

MIRANDA
O Ma'am, most heedfully!

PROSPERA
Perverting my
Upstanding studies, now his slandering
And bile-dipped brush did paint a faithless portrait—
His sister, a practicer of black arts!;
A demon; not a woman, nay—a witch!
And he full-knowing others of my sex
Have burned for no less! The flames now fanned,
My counselors turned against me—
Dost thou hear?

MIRANDA
Your tale, ma'am, would cure deafness.

PROSPERA
To credit his own lie he did believe he was indeed the Duke;
Confederates wi' the King of Naples
To give him annual tribute, and bend

My dukedom yet unbow'd
To most ignoble stooping.

MIRANDA
    O the heavens!

PROSPERA
    Now the condition.
The King of Naples, being an enemy
To me inveterate, hearkens my brother's suit;
Which was, that he,
Should presently eradicate me and mine
Out of the dukedom and confer fair Milan
With all the honors on my brother: whereon,
One midnight did Antonio open
The gates of Milan, and, i' the dead of darkness,
The ministers for the purpose hurried thence
Me and thy crying self.

MIRANDA
    Wherefore did they not

That hour destroy us?

PROSPERA
    Dear, they durst not,
So dear the love my people bore me.
In few, they hurried us aboard a bark,
Bore us some leagues to sea, where they prepared
A rotten carcass of a boat not rigg'd,
Nor tackle, sail, nor mast; the very rats
Instinctively had quit it: there they hoist us,
To cry to the sea that roar'd to us, to sigh
To the winds whose pity, sighing back again,
Did us but loving wrong.

MIRANDA
    Alack, what trouble was I then to you!

PROSPERA takes her daughter into her arms.

PROSPERA
    O, a cherubim

Thou wast that did preserve me! Thou didst smile.
Infused with a fortitude from heaven, which raised in me
An undergoing stomach, to bear up
Against what should ensue.

MIRANDA
How came we ashore?

PROSPERA
By Providence divine.
Some food we had and some fresh water that
A noble Neapolitan, Gonzalo,
Out of his charity, did give us, with
Rich garments, linens, stuffs and necessaries,
Which since have steaded much. So, of his gentleness,
Knowing I loved my books, he furnish'd me
From mine own library with volumes that
I prize above my dukedom.

MIRANDA
Would I might
But ever see that man!

PROSPERA
Now I arise.

MIRANDA
I pray you, ma'am,
For still 'tis beating in my mind, your reason
For raising this sea-storm?

PROSPERA
By accident most strange, bountiful Fortune,
Now my dear lady, hath mine enemies
Brought to this shore.

MIRANDA begins to question, but PROSPERA has taken her
staff and with a slight movement halts her speech.

PROSPERA (CONT'D)
Here cease more questions.
Thou art inclined to sleep. 'Tis a good dulness,
And give it way: I know thou canst not choose.

MIRANDA falls asleep.

EXT. CELL COURTYARD - DAY

PROSPERA exits from her cave into the courtyard and kneels before a half-circle pool of water. As she begins to speak, we see her reflection evolve into the arrival of ARIEL, emerging from clouds, deep in the pool.

> PROSPERA
> Come away, servant, come. I am ready now.
> Approach, my Ariel, come.

The spirit, ARIEL, is the essence of energy, composed of light filtered through vibrations and patterns of air, fire, and water.

He is an androgynous spirit that can transform his physical presence with a flick of PROSPERA'S command or his own quicksilver change of mood and passion.

He appears in or as the elements of nature, i.e., a human form that is filled at different times with storm-wind, fire, clouds, butterflies, bees, fireflies, etc.

With his mood swings, colors and patterns run up and down his form, and his size and shape can expand, contract, split, and multiply, freely moving in and around the environment.

He is only visible to PROSPERA and, of course, to the audience.

> ARIEL
> All hail, great master! Grave dame, hail! I come
> To answer thy best pleasure; be't to fly,
> To swim, to dive into the fire, to ride
> On the curl'd clouds, to thy strong bidding task
> Ariel and all his quality.

Like a blowhole, the water from the pool shoots into the air with fragments of ARIEL'S body caught in the droplets and mist.

ARIEL continues to speak through the water. The atmosphere around PROSPERA is charged and changed.

> PROSPERA
> Hast thou, spirit,
> Perform'd, to point, the tempest that I bade thee?

The following depiction of the shipwreck is from ARIEL'S point of view.

Images we have previously seen tumble at us in fragmented snippets
with the supernatural presence of ARIEL, the major player.

ARIEL

      To every article.
I boarded the King's ship. Now on the beak,
Now in the waist, the deck, in every cabin,
I flamed amazement: sometime I'd divide
And burn in many places; the fire and cracks
Of sulphurous roaring the most mighty Neptune
Seem to besiege and make his bold waves tremble;
Yea, his dread trident shake.

PROSPERA

      My brave spirit!
Who was so firm, so constant, that this coil
Would not infect his reason?

ARIEL

      Not a soul
But felt a fever of the mad and play'd
Some tricks of desperation. The king's son, Ferdinand,
With hair up-staring—
Was the first man that leap'd; cried, "Hell is empty
And all the devils are here."

PROSPERA

      Why that's my spirit!
But was not this nigh shore?

ARIEL

      Close by, my master.

PROSPERA

But are they, Ariel, safe?

CUT TO: EXT. A BEACH - DAY

ALONSO, ANTONIO, SEBASTIAN, and GONZALO slowly, miraculously rise out of the ocean and, in a daze, walk onto the beach. (In shooting this image, the actors will walk backward into the ocean and the footage will be played in reverse so that their garments will appear to be dry as they arise out of the sea.)

> ARIEL (CONT'D O.C.)
> Not a hair perish'd.
> On their sustaining garments not a blemish,
> But fresher than before: and, as thou badest me,
> In troops I have dispersed them 'bout the isle.

CUT TO: EXT. THE CORAL FLATS - DAY

FERDINAND sits on the coral rocks, his arms wrapped tightly about his knees.

> ARIEL (CONT'D O.C.)
> The King's son have I landed by himself,
> Whom I left cooling of the air with sighs
> In an odd angle of the isle and sitting,
> His arms in this sad knot.

46

> PROSPERA (O.C.)
> Of the King's ship, the Mariners, say how thou hast disposed,
> And all the rest o' the fleet.

CUT TO: EXT. HARBOR - DAY

The KING'S ship peacefully sits in a tranquil bay. There is no sign of the damage that it went through in the tempest.

> ARIEL (O.C.)
> Safely in harbor
> Is the King's ship; in the deep nook, there she's hid;
> The Mariners all under hatches stow'd,

CUT TO: EXT. CELL COURTYARD - DAY

> ARIEL (CONT'D)
> Who, with a charm, I have left asleep.

PROSPERA is delighted with ARIEL'S report but an urgent seriousness suddenly overtakes her.

> PROSPERA
> Ariel, thy charge
> Exactly is perform'd: but there's more work.
> What is the time o' the day?

> ARIEL
> Past the mid season.

> PROSPERA
> At least two glasses. The time 'twixt six and now
> Must by us both be spent most preciously.

> ARIEL
> Is there more toil? Since thou dost give me pains,
> Let me remember thee what thou hast promised,
> Which is not yet perform'd me.

> PROSPERA
> How now? Moody?
> What is't thou canst demand?

> ARIEL
> My liberty.

> PROSPERA
> Before the time be out? No more!

PROSPERA flicks ARIEL away, turns to leave but is stopped dead-on by the obsequious spirit who clings to her foot.

ARIEL
    I prithee,
Remember I have done thee worthy service,
Thou didst promise to bate me a full year.

PROSPERA
    Dost thou forget
From what a torment I did free thee?

ARIEL
    No.

PROSPERA
    Thou dost.

ARIEL
    I do not, ma'am.

PROSPERA
    Thou liest, malignant thing! Hast thou forgot
The foul witch Sycorax, hast thou forgot her?

ARIEL
No, ma'am.

PROSPERA
Thou hast. Where was she born? Speak!
Tell me.

ARIEL
Ma'am, in Algiers.

PROSPERA
    O, was she so? I must
Once in a month recount what thou hast been,
Which thou forget'st. This damn'd witch Sycorax,
For mischiefs manifold and sorceries terrible
To enter human hearing, from Algiers,
Thou know'st, was banish'd. Is not this true?

ARIEL
Ay, ma'am.

PROSPERA
    This blue-eyed hag was hither brought with child
And here was left by the sailors. Thou, my slave,
As thou report'st thyself, wast then her servant.
And, for thou wast a spirit too delicate

To act her earthy and abhorr'd commands,
           she did confine thee
Into a cloven pine; within which rift
Imprison'd thou didst painfully remain
A dozen years; within which space she died
And left thee there; where thou didst vent thy groans.

As ARIEL listens to this familiar retelling of his early days, we will see his image melting into a hole in a great old pine tree.

His tortured expressions evolve as the bark of the tree closes in on his face.

Back to PROSPERA.

PROSPERA (CONT'D)
Then was this island—not honor'd with a human shape,
Save Caliban her son. Thou best know'st
What torment I did find thee in; thy groans
Did make wolves howl and penetrate the breasts
Of ever angry bears: it was mine art,
When I arrived and heard thee, that made gape
The pine, and let thee out.

ARIEL
      I thank thee, master.

PROSPERA
If thou more murmur'st, I will rend an oak
And peg thee in his knotty entrails till
Thou hast howl'd away twelve winters.

ARIEL
    Pardon, master.
I will be correspondent to command
And do my spiriting gently.

PROSPERA
    Do so, and after two days
I will discharge thee.

ARIEL
    That's my noble master!
What shall I do? Say what? What shall I do?

PROSPERA
Go make thyself like a nymph o' the sea. Be subject
To no sight but thine and mine, invisible
To every eyeball else. Go! Hence with diligence!

ARIEL flies off like a mad hornet, and the atmosphere around
PROSPERA is restored to "reality."

INT. PROSPERA'S CELL - DAY

A hand softly glides over the face of the sleeping MIRANDA.

PROSPERA
Awake, dear heart, awake! Thou hast slept well.
Awake!

MIRANDA
The strangeness of your story put
Heaviness in me.

PROSPERA
     Shake it off. Come on.
We'll visit Caliban, my slave, who never
Yields us kind answer.

CUT TO: EXT. THE GARDEN OF PROSPERA'S CELL - DAY

The dialogue continues as MIRANDA and PROSPERA emerge out of the caves and into the garden of the walled cell.

MIRANDA
     'Tis a villain, ma'am,
I do not love to look on.

PROSPERA
     But, as 'tis,
We cannot miss him. He does make our fire,
Fetch in our wood, and serves in offices
That profit us.

They will continue up the lava steps through wild and exotic fruit trees and flowers that have clearly been born of the organic alchemist's experiments with nature.

Two giant walls of white coral rock enclose the garden and inner sanctum of PROSPERA'S dwelling, protecting it from the harsh winds that blow from the sea.

EXT. CLIFF TRAIL - DAY

PROSPERA and MIRANDA make their way down the high cliff trail.

EXT. BLACK VOLCANIC LAVA MOUNDS - DAY

An endless vista of petrified black lava mounds reaching all the way to huge cliffs hanging over an angry sea.

In the distance, we see PROSPERA and MIRANDA crossing the desolate and harsh terrain. They finally arrive at a particularly high mound in an infinite vista of black lava rock.

> PROSPERA
> What, ho! Slave! Caliban!

PROSPERA bangs her staff on the ground, causing a loud, reverberating thud.

> PROSPERA (CONT'D)
> Thou earth, thou! Speak.

> CALIBAN (O.C.)
> There's wood enough within!

> PROSPERA
> Come forth, I say!

CUT TO: INT. BELOW THE LAVA MOUND, CALIBAN'S HOLE - DAY

CALIBAN is the antithesis of ARIEL. He is earth. He is the island.

Most of his skin resembles the bluish, black, and clay-red earth, its texture made of fossilized shells and hardened lava. The rest of his body is textured with maplike shapes of white skin.

His head, chest, and limbs are carved with random curse words learned from his master, PROSPERA—some formed as angry raised scars, some as tattoos made with squid ink and natural dyes.

One of his eyes is a watery blue, and between his fingers stretch hints of webbing.

As PROSPERA orders him to come forth, CALIBAN grumbles as he gnaws upon a hairy root.

> CALIBAN
> I must eat my dinner!

> PROSPERA (O.C.)
> There's other business for thee.
> Come, thou tortoise! When?

EXT. BLACK VOLCANIC LAVA MOUNDS - DAY

PROSPERA calls to the recalcitrant CALIBAN.

PROSPERA
Thou poisonous slave, got by the devil himself
Upon thy wicked dam, come forth!

Finally, CALIBAN emerges out of a deep crevice in the earth.

Standing high above mother and daughter, his imposing presence
looms as a silhouette against the bright sky.

CALIBAN
As wicked dew as e'er my mother brush'd
With raven's feather from unwholesome fen
Drop on you both! A southwest blow on ye
And blister you all o'er!

Raising her staff, PROSPERA causes CALIBAN to crumble as her
magical power mentally and physically torments him.

PROSPERA
For this, be sure, tonight thou shalt have cramps,
Side-stitches that shall pen thy breath up. Urchins
Shall work all exercise on thee; thou shalt be pinch'd
As thick as honeycomb, each pinch more stinging
Than bees that made 'em.

CALIBAN
(defiantly)
      This island's mine by Sycorax my mother,
Which thou tak'st from me. When thou camest first,
Thou strok'st me and madest much of me; wouldst give me
Water with berries in't; and teach me how
To name the bigger light, and how the less,
That burn by day and night. And then I loved thee
And show'd thee all the qualities o' th' isle,
The fresh springs, brine-pits, barren place and fertile.
Cursed be I that did so! All the charms
Of Sycorax—toads, beetles, bats, light on you!
For I am all the subjects that you have,
Which first was mine own king; and here you sty me
In this hard rock, whiles you do keep from me
The rest o' th' island.

PROSPERA
      Thou most lying slave,
Whom stripes may move, not kindness! I have used thee,

With humane care, and lodged thee
In mine own cell, till thou didst seek to violate
The honor of my child.

CALIBAN dodges past PROSPERA and leans salaciously toward
MIRANDA.

CALIBAN
O ho, O ho! Would't had been done!
Thou didst prevent me; I had peopled else
This isle with Calibans.

MIRANDA
    Abhorrèd slave,
Which any print of goodness wilt not take,
I pitied thee, took pains to make thee speak.

CALIBAN
You taught me language, and my profit on't
Is, I know how to curse. The red plague rid you

For learning me your language!

PROSPERA
    Hagseed, hence!
Fetch us in fuel. Shrug'st thou, malice?
If thou neglect'st or dost unwillingly
What I command, I'll rack thee with old cramps,
Fill all thy bones with aches, make thee roar
That beasts shall tremble at thy din.

CALIBAN
    No, pray thee.
(to himself)
I must obey. Her art is of such power.

PROSPERA
    So, slave; Hence!

Defeated, CALIBAN grumbles as he moves off in the direction of
PROSPERA'S cell.

EXT. BLACK CORAL, ROCKY SHORELINE - DAY

FERDINAND sits as we saw him before, huddled in a tight ball, on the rocks at the edge of the sea. He is a young prince of nineteen years whose handsome, aristocratic face is dark with the assumed loss of his father, the KING, and the rest of the shipmates.

The nymph, ARIEL, sings. FERDINAND only hears the haunting voice and is drawn to it. Again, we can see ARIEL, but FERDINAND cannot. ARIEL'S face and body will move through the various pools of water and through the leaves of the trees and rocky cliffs during the song:

> ARIEL
> (singing)
> *Come unto these darkened sands,*
> *And then take hands.*
> *Curtsied when you have and kiss'd*
> *The wild waves whist,*
> *Foot it featly here and there;*

> *And, sweet sprites, the burden bear.*
> *Hark, hark!*

> *Hark, hark!*
> *The watchdogs bark.*
> *Hark, hark!*
> *The watchdogs bark.*

During the song FERDINAND rises as if in a dream and follows the drift of the music and the strands of glowing light that are the almost transparent feminine form of ARIEL as a SEA NYMPH.

> FERDINAND
> Where should this music be? I' th' air or th' earth?
> It sounds no more; and sure, it waits upon
> Some god o' th' island.
> Thence I have follow'd it,
> Or it hath drawn me rather; but 'tis gone.
> No, it begins again.

EXT. FOREST TRAIL BY THE SEA - DAY

ARIEL/NYMPH appears and disappears through the wet leaves and puddles on the meandering path. FERDINAND is led in and out of dark shadows and blinding light until he is once again on an open beach, which is backed by high rock cliffs.

>   ARIEL
>   (singing)
>   *Full fathom five thy father lies;*
>   *Of his bones are coral made;*
>   *Those are pearls that were his eyes;*
>   *Nothing of him that doth fade*

But doth suffer a sea change
Into something rich and strange.
Sea-nymphs hourly ring his knell:

Now I hear them—.

FERDINAND
The ballad does remember my drown'd father.
This is no mortal business, nor no sound
That the earth owes. I hear it now above me.

Come unto these
darkened sands
And then take hands

*Curtsied when you have
and kiss'd
The wild waves whist*

Full fathom five
thy father lies
Of his bones are
coral made

EXT. ROCKY SHORELINE/WOODS - DAY

Hidden by the trees on a high mound, FERDINAND is being watched by PROSPERA and MIRANDA.

PROSPERA
The fringèd curtains of thine eye advance
And say what thou seest yond.

MIRANDA
    What is't? A spirit?

PROSPERA
No, child; it eats and sleeps and hath such senses
As we have, such. This gallant which thou seest
Was in the wreck.

MIRANDA
    I might call him
A thing divine, for nothing natural
I ever saw so noble.

She breaks away from PROSPERA and moves for a closer look at FERDINAND.

ARIEL flies to PROSPERA'S side.

PROSPERA
(aside)
    It goes on, I see,
As my soul prompts it. Spirit, fine spirit! I'll free thee
Within two days for this.

MIRANDA scrambles down the hill and stands before FERDINAND.

Startled by her sudden presence and the fact that he is not alone on the island, he fumbles for words.

FERDINAND
    Most sure, the goddess
On whom these airs attend! Vouchsafe my prayer
May know if you remain upon this island,
And that you will some good instruction give
How I may bear me here. My prime request,
Which I do last pronounce, is, (O you wonder!)
If you be maid or no?

MIRANDA
    No wonder, sir,
But certainly a maid.

FERDINAND
    My language! Heavens!
I am the best of them that speak this speech,
Were I but where 'tis spoken.

PROSPERA appears behind him.

Her low voice challenges his assumption.

PROSPERA
    How? The best?
What wert thou, if the King of Naples heard thee?

Surprised, FERDINAND turns to face PROSPERA, whom he could easily mistake for a man, not only because of the timbre of her voice, but by her clothes and the cut of her hair, which are both somewhat masculine in appearance.

FERDINAND
A single thing, as I am now, that wonders
To hear thee speak of Naples. He does hear me;
And that he does I weep: myself am Naples,
Who with mine eyes, never since at ebb, beheld
The King my father wreck'd.

MIRANDA
Alack, for mercy!

FERDINAND
Yes, faith, and all his lords.

MIRANDA and FERDINAND stand as if in a trance, enamored with one another.

PROSPERA turns to ARIEL, amused.

PROSPERA
At the first sight
They have changed eyes. Delicate Ariel,
I'll set thee free for this.
(to FERDINAND)
A word, good sir.
I fear you have done yourself some wrong. A word!

MIRANDA
(to herself)
Why speaks my mother so ungently? This
Is the second man that e'er I saw, the first
That e'er I sigh'd for.

PROSPERA
(to herself)
They are both in either's powers; but this swift business
I must uneasy make, lest too light winning
Make the prize light.
(harshly to FERDINAND)
One word more! I charge thee
That thou attend me. Thou dost here usurp
The name thou ow'st not, and hast put thyself
Upon this island as a spy, to win it
From me, the sovereign on't.

FERDINAND
No, as I am a man.

MIRANDA
There's nothing ill can dwell in such a temple.

PROSPERA
Follow me.
(to MIRANDA)
Speak not you for him; he's a traitor.
(to FERDINAND)
Come! I'll manacle thy neck and feet together;
Sea-water shalt thou drink. Follow!

FERDINAND
No. I will resist such entertainment till
Mine enemy has more pow'r.

He draws his sword, wheels around toward PROSPERA, and is charmed from moving.

PROSPERA'S magic, emanating from her staff, surrounds FERDINAND with threatening sounds and movement.

In a moment he is surprised to discover that his challenger is a woman and the mother of MIRANDA.

MIRANDA
O dear mother,
Make not too rash a trial of him, for
He's gentle and not fearful.

PROSPERA
What, I say,
My foot my tutor?
(to FERDINAND)
Put thy sword up, traitor—
For I can here disarm thee with this stick
And make thy weapon drop.

MIRANDA
Beseech you, mother.

PROSPERA
Hence! Hang not on my garments.

MIRANDA
Ma'am, have pity.
I'll be his surety.

PROSPERA
Silence! One word more
Shall make me chide thee, if not hate thee.
Thou think'st there is no more such shapes as he,
Having seen but him and Caliban. Foolish child!
To th' most of men this is a Caliban

And they to him are angels.

MIRANDA

    My affections
Are then most humble; I have no ambition
To see a goodlier man.

PROSPERA

(to FERDINAND)

Come on, obey!
Thy nerves are in their infancy again
And have no vigor in them.

As if the wind were knocked out of him, FERDINAND slowly recovers and begins to move.

FERDINAND

    So they are.
My spirits, as in a dream, are all bound up.
My father's loss, the weakness which I feel,
The wreck of all my friends, nor this dame's threats,
To whom I am subdued, are but light to me,
Might I but through my prison once a day
Behold this maid. All corners else o' the earth

Let liberty make use of. Space enough
Have I in such a prison.

PROSPERA

(aside)

It works.

(to FERDINAND)

Come on.

She leads MIRANDA and FERDINAND up the steep path of the cliff.

PROSPERA (CONT'D)

(to ARIEL)

Thou hast done well, fine Ariel!
Hark what thou else shalt do me.

MIRANDA

(turning to FERDINAND)

    Be of comfort.
My mother's of a better nature, sir,
Than she appears by speech.

PROSPERA

(to ARIEL)

    Thou shalt be free
As mountain winds; but then exactly do
All points of my command.

ARIEL

    To th' syllable.

PROSPERA

(to FERDINAND)

Come, follow.

(to MIRANDA)

Speak not for him.

EXT. BARREN DESERT LANDSCAPE - DAY

The surviving court trudges through the landscape in search of any of the survivors.

KING ALONSO leads, followed by GONZALO and the mocking duo, ANTONIO and SEBASTIAN.

> **GONZALO**
> Beseech you, sir, be merry; you have cause,
> (So have we all,) of joy; for our escape
> Is much beyond our loss. But for the miracle,
> I mean our preservation, few in millions
> Can speak like us. Then wisely, good sir, weigh
> Our sorrow with our comfort.

> **ALONSO**
> *(annoyed)*
> >   Prithee, peace.

> **SEBASTIAN**
> *(aside to ANTONIO)*
> He receives comfort like cold porridge.

> **ANTONIO**
> Look, he's winding up the watch of his wit; by and by
> it will strike.

> **GONZALO**
> Sir—

> **SEBASTIAN**
> *(aside to ANTONIO)*
> One. Tell.

> **GONZALO**
> When every grief is entertain'd that's offer'd,
> Comes to the entertainer—

> **SEBASTIAN**
> A dollar.

GONZALO turns back to SEBASTIAN.

> **GONZALO**
> Dolor comes to him, indeed. You have spoken truer than you
> purposed.

> **SEBASTIAN**
> You have taken it wiselier than I meant you should.

GONZALO
(catching up to the KING)
Therefore, my lord—

ANTONIO
Fie, what a spendthrift is he of his tongue!

ALONSO stops in his tracks and turns to GONZALO.

ALONSO
I prithee, spare.

GONZALO
Well, I have done. But yet,—

SEBASTIAN
He will be talking.

GONZALO
Though this island seem to be desert—

ANTONIO
Ha, ha, ha!

GONZALO
Uninhabitable and almost inaccessible,—

SEBASTIAN
Yet—

GONZALO
Yet—

ANTONIO
He could not miss't.

GONZALO
The air breathes upon us here most sweetly.

SEBASTIAN
As if it had lungs, and rotten ones.

ANTONIO
Or as 'twere perfumed by a fen.

GONZALO
Here is everything advantageous to life.

ANTONIO
True; save means to live.

SEBASTIAN
Of that there's none, or little.

GONZALO
How lush and lusty the grass looks! How green!

ANTONIO
The ground indeed is tawny.

SEBASTIAN
With an eye of green in't.

GONZALO
But the rarity of it is—which is indeed almost beyond
credit—that our garments, being, as they were,
drenched in the sea, are now as fresh as when we put them on

first in Afric, in Tunis, at the marriage of your fair
daughter Claribel to the King of Tunis.

ALONSO

You cram these words into mine ears against
The stomach of my sense. Would I had never
Married my daughter there! For, coming thence,
My son is lost; and, in my rate, she too,
Who is so far from Italy removed
I ne'er again shall see her. O thou mine heir
Of Naples and of Milan, what strange fish
Hath made his meal on thee?

ANTONIO

    Sir, he may live.
I saw him beat the surges under him,
And ride upon their backs. I not doubt
He came alive to land.

ALONSO

    No, no, he's gone.

SEBASTIAN

(to ALONSO)
Sir, you may thank yourself for this great loss,
That would not bless our Europe with your daughter,
But rather lose her to an African.

ALONSO

    Prithee, peace.

SEBASTIAN

    We have lost your son, I fear, forever.
The fault's your own.

ALONSO

    So is the dear'st o' the loss.

ALONSO is so shaken with the loss of his son, he falters in his steps.

GONZALO comes to his aid. He then sternly admonishes SEBASTIAN.

GONZALO

My lord Sebastian,
The truth you speak doth lack some gentleness
And time to speak it in. You rub the sore,
When you should bring the plaster.

SEBASTIAN

    Very well.

ANTONIO

And most like a surgeon.

GONZALO

(back to the KING)
It is foul weather in us all, good sir,
When you are cloudy.

SEBASTIAN

(aside to ANTONIO)
Foul weather?

ANTONIO

(aside to SEBASTIAN)
    Very foul.

EXT. OPEN RED ROCKY LANDSCAPE (NEAR THE OCEAN) - DAY

The skies are overcast with great clouds. CALIBAN crosses with an armful of wood.

CALIBAN

All the infections that the sun sucks up
From bogs, fens, flats, on Prospera fall and make her
By inchmeal a disease!

A rumble of thunder. He drops the wood.

CALIBAN (CONT'D)

Her spirits hear me,
And yet I needs must curse.

He tries to gather his bundle back together.

CALIBAN (CONT'D)

But for every trifle are they set upon me;
Sometime like apes that mow and chatter at me
And after bite me; then like hedgehogs which
Lie tumbling in my barefoot way and mount
Their pricks at my footfall; sometime am I
All wound with adders who with cloven tongues
Do hiss me into madness.

TRINCULO, the KING'S fool, walks alone in the distance, turning in all directions, clearly lost.

He is played as an Italian scoundrel from Naples with a flair for commedia. Nervous, twitchy, like a sewer rat, he tries to be brave but is easily terrified.

CALIBAN (CONT'D)
Lo, now, lo!
Here comes a spirit of hers, and to torment me
For bringing wood in slowly. I'll fall flat.
Perchance he will not mind me.

He falls to the ground and pulls an animal skin blanket over his body to hide from TRINCULO.

TRINCULO
Here's neither bush nor shrub, to bear off
Any weather at all, and another storm brewing;
I hear it sing i' the wind. Yond same black cloud,
Yond huge one, looks like a foul bombard that
Would shed his liquor. If it should thunder as
It did before, I know not where to hide my head.
Yond same cloud cannot choose but fall by pailfuls.

He trips over the body of CALIBAN and carefully lifts the blanket to inspect.

TRINCULO (CONT'D)
What have we here? A man or a fish? Dead or alive?

Sniffing the immobile body, he instantly backs off at the foul smell.

TRINCULO (CONT'D)
A fish! He smells like a fish; a very ancient
And fishlike smell. A strange fish!
Were I in England now, as once I was, and had but
This fish painted, not a holiday fool there but
Would give a piece of silver. There would this
Monster make a man; any strange beast there makes a man.
When they will not give a penny to relieve a lame beggar,
They will lay out ten to see a dead Indian.

Now he thoroughly, but cautiously, investigates the body.

TRINCULO (CONT'D)
Legged like a man and his fins like arms!

Upon touching CALIBAN...

TRINCULO (CONT'D)
Warm o' my troth!
I do now let loose my opinion, hold it no longer.
This is no fish, but an islander, that hath
Lately suffered by a thunderbolt.

A loud rumble of thunder sends a shudder through TRINCULO'S system.

TRINCULO (CONT'D)
Alas, the storm is come again!
My best way is to creep under his gaberdine;
There is no other shelter hereabouts.

With much disdain, he gingerly picks back the animal hide and crawls under.

TRINCULO (CONT'D)
Misery acquaints a man with strange bedfellows.

EXT. RIDGE, RED ROCKY LANDSCAPE (NEAR OCEAN) - DAY

From over a ridge appears the drunken butler, STEPHANO.

Bottle in hand, he sings with gusto a bawdy sailor song.

STEPHANO
(sings)
The master, the swabber, the boatswain, and I,
The gunner and his mate,
Loved Mall, Meg and Marian and Margery,
But none of us cared for Kate;
For she had a tongue with a tang,
Would cry to a sailor, "Go hang!"
She loved not the savor of tar nor of pitch;
Yet a tailor might scratch her where'er she did itch:
Then to sea, boys, and let her go hang!
Then to sea, boys, and let her go hang!

As he takes a swig he stumbles down the ridge hill, coming close to the mound that is CALIBAN and TRINCULO.

CALIBAN
Do not torment me! O!

STEPHANO is taken aback at the giant mystery blob before him.

From under the blanket protrude CALIBAN'S two muscular, clay-covered legs and TRINCULO'S two skinny legs.

STEPHANO
What's the matter? Have we devils here?
Do you put tricks upon's with savages and
Men of Inde, ha? I have not scaped drowning
To be afeard now of your four legs.

CALIBAN
The spirit torments me. O!

STEPHANO
This is some monster of the isle with four legs,
Who hath got, as I take it, an ague.
Where the devil should he learn our language?

I will give him some relief, if it be but for that.
If I can recover him, and keep him tame and get
To Naples with him, he's a present for any emperor.

STEPHANO bends his body over what appears to be the front of the creature.

He lifts the blanket, raises its head, and attempts to pour the liquor into his mouth.

CALIBAN
Do not torment me, prithee; I'll bring my wood home faster.

STEPHANO
He's in his fit now and does not talk after the wisest.
He shall taste of my bottle. Come on your ways,
Open your mouth. This will shake your shaking,
I can tell you, and that soundly.
(*gives CALIBAN drink*)
You cannot tell who's your friend. Open your chaps again.

TRINCULO
(*under the blanket and to himself*)

Misery acquaints a man with strange bedfellows

I should know that voice. It should be—but he is drowned; and these are devils. O, defend me!

STEPHANO pops his head up to see where the voice came from.

STEPHANO

Four legs and two voices—a most delicate monster! Come.
(gives CALIBAN more drink)
Amen! I will pour some in thy other mouth.

TRINCULO

Stephano!

STEPHANO

Doth thy other mouth call me? Mercy, mercy!
This is a devil, and no monster: I will leave him.

TRINCULO

Stephano! If thou beest Stephano, touch me
and speak to me; for I am Trinculo—be not
afeard—thy good friend Trinculo.

STEPHANO

If thou beest Trinculo, come forth. I'll pull thee
by the lesser legs. If any be Trinculo's legs, these are they.
(draws him out from under CALIBAN'S blanket)
Thou art very Trinculo indeed!
How camest thou to be the siege of this mooncalf?
Can he vent Trinculos?

TRINCULO

I took him to be killed with a thunder-stroke.
But art thou not drowned, Stephano?
I hid me under the dead mooncalf's gaberdine
for fear of the storm.
And art thou living, Stephano?
O Stephano, two Neapolitans 'scaped!

STEPHANO

(about to vomit)
Prithee, do not turn me about; my stomach is
not constant.

CALIBAN has been watching these two reunite.

He is still cautious but also curious about such strange excitable beings.

The two "clowns" are your classic commedia duo, with plenty of low brow twist and physical humor.

CALIBAN
(to himself)
These be fine things, an if they be not sprites.
That's a brave god and bears celestial liquor.
I will kneel to him.

STEPHANO
How didst thou 'scape? How camest thou hither?
Swear by this bottle how thou cam'st hither.
I escaped upon a butt of sack which the sailors
heaved o'erboard.

CALIBAN
I'll swear upon that bottle to be thy true subject,
for the liquor is not earthly.

STEPHANO
Here! Swear then how thou escapedst.

TRINCULO
Swum ashore, man, like a duck. I can swim
like a duck, I'll be sworn.

STEPHANO
Here, kiss the book.

Gives him drink and watches the liquor flow down TRINCULO'S extended gullet.

STEPHANO (CONT'D)
Though thou canst swim like a duck, thou art
made like a goose.

TRINCULO
O Stephano. Hast any more of this?

STEPHANO
The whole butt, man.
(turning to CALIBAN)
How now, mooncalf! How does thine ague?

CALIBAN
Hast thou not dropp'd from heaven?

STEPHANO
Out o' th' moon, I do assure thee. I was the
Man i' the Moon when time was.

CALIBAN
I have seen thee in her and I do adore thee.

STEPHANO
Come, swear to that; kiss the book.
(gives him drink)
Swear.
(CALIBAN drinks)

TRINCULO
By this good light, this is a very shallow monster!
I afeard of him? A very weak monster!
The Man i' the Moon! A most poor credulous monster!

CALIBAN
I'll show thee every fertile inch o' th' island;
And I will kiss thy foot.
I prithee, be my god.

STEPHANO
Come on then. Down, and swear!

TRINCULO
I shall laugh myself to death at this
puppy-headed monster. A most scurvy monster!
I could find in my heart to beat him—

STEPHANO
Come, kiss.

TRINCULO
But that the poor monster's in drink.

CALIBAN
I'll show thee the best springs; I'll pluck thee berries;
I'll fish for thee and get thee wood enough.
A plague upon the tyrant that I serve!
I'll bear her no more sticks, but follow thee,
Thou wondrous man.

TRINCULO
A most ridiculous monster, to make a wonder of a poor drunkard!

CALIBAN
I prithee, let me bring thee where crabs grow;
And I with my long nails will dig thee pignuts,

Show thee a jay's nest, and instruct thee how
To snare the nimble marmoset. I'll bring thee
To clust'ring filberts, and sometimes I'll get thee
Young scamels from the rock. Wilt thou go with me?

STEPHANO
I prithee now, lead the way without any more talking.
Trinculo, the King and all our company else being drowned,
we will inherit here.

CALIBAN
(sing drunkenly)
Farewell master; farewell, farewell!

TRINCULO
A howling monster! A drunken monster!

CALIBAN
No more dams I'll make for fish
Nor fetch in firing
At requiring,
Nor scrape trencher, nor wash dish
'Ban, 'Ban, Ca—Caliban
Has a new master. Get a new man!

Freedom, high day! High day, freedom! Freedom,
high day, high day freedom!

STEPHANO
O brave monster! Lead the way.

EXT. A HIGH RIDGE OVER THE SEA - DAY

The three drunken sots madly dance along the high ridge over the sea,
their bodies silhouetted against the sky.

90

Freedom, high day!
High day, freedom!

O brave monster!
Lead the way.

EXT. CANYON AND STEEP PATH - DAY

FERDINAND collects logs and kindling, strapping the load to his back to bring to PROSPERA'S cell.

> **FERDINAND**
> This my mean task
> Would be as heavy to me as odious, but
> The mistress which I serve quickens what's dead
> And makes my labors pleasures.

For a moment he pauses, and lowers the heavy burden to rest and day-dreams about MIRANDA.

> **FERDINAND (CONT'D)**
> O, she is
> Ten times more gentle than her mother's crabbed,
> And she's composed of harshness! I must remove
> Some thousands of these logs and pile them up,
> Upon a sore injunction. My sweet mistress

Weeps when she sees me work, and says, such baseness
Had never like executor. I forget;
But these sweet thoughts do even refresh my labors,
Most busiest, when I work.

He struggles to pick up the logs and gather them in a bundle.

MIRANDA approaches while PROSPERA observes at a distance, unseen.

> **MIRANDA**
> Alas, now, pray you,
> Work not so hard! I would the lightning had
> Burnt up those logs that you are enjoin'd to pile!
> Pray, set it down and rest you. When this burns,
> 'Twill weep for having wearied you. My mother
> Is hard at study; pray now, rest yourself;
> She's safe for these three hours.

FERDINAND keeps on with the task.

FERDINAND
 O most dear mistress,
The sun will set before I shall discharge
What I must strive to do.

MIRANDA
 If you'll sit down,
I'll bear your logs the while. Pray, give me that;
I'll carry it to the pile.

She grabs the logs and he grabs them back.

It is clear that MIRANDA *is much more athletic and used to moving on the wild terrain.*

FERDINAND
 No, precious creature,
I had rather crack my sinews, break my back,

Than you should such dishonor undergo,
While I sit lazy by.

MIRANDA
 It would become me
As well as it does you; and I should do it
With much more ease; for my good will is to it,
And yours it is against.

PROSPERA
(aside)
Poor worm, thou art infected!
This visitation shows it.

MIRANDA
 You look wearily.

FERDINAND

No, noble mistress; 'tis fresh morning with me
When you are by at night. I do beseech you—
What is your name?

MIRANDA

     Miranda. O my mother,
I have broke your hest to say so!

FERDINAND

     Admired Miranda!
Indeed the top of admiration! worth
What's dearest to the world! Full many a lady
I have eyed with best regard and many a time
The harmony of their tongues hath into bondage
Brought my too diligent ear. For several virtues
Have I liked several women; never any
With so full soul, but some defect in her
Did quarrel with the noblest grace she owed
And put it to the foil. But you, O you,
So perfect and so peerless, are created
Of every creature's best!

MIRANDA

     I know only
One more of my sex; no young woman's face
Remember, save, from my glass, mine own.
Nor have I seen more that I may call men
Than you, good friend: how features are abroad,
I am skilless of; but, by my modesty,
        I would not wish
Any companion in the world but you,
Nor can imagination form a shape,
Besides yourself, to like of. But I prattle
Something too wildly and my mother's precepts
I therein do forget.

FERDINAND

     I am in my condition
A prince, Miranda; I do think, a king;
I would, not so. Hear my soul speak!
The very instant that I saw you, did
My heart fly to your service; there resides,
To make me slave to it; and for your sake
Am I this patient log-man.

MIRANDA
>Do you love me?

FERDINAND
O heaven, O earth, bear witness to this sound, I
Beyond all limit of what else i' th' world
Do love, prize, honor you.

MIRANDA
>I am a fool
To weep at what I am glad of.

FERDINAND
>Wherefore weep you?

MIRANDA
At mine unworthiness that dare not offer
What I desire to give, and much less take
What I shall die to want. But this is trifling;
And all the more it seeks to hide itself,
The bigger bulk it shows. Hence, bashful cunning,
And prompt me, plain and holy innocence!
I am your wife, if you will marry me;
If not, I'll die your maid. To be your fellow
You may deny me; but I'll be your servant,
Whether you will or no.

FERDINAND
>My mistress, dearest.
And I thus humble ever.

MIRANDA
>My husband, then?

FERDINAND
>Ay, with a heart as willing
As bondage e'er of freedom. Here's my hand.

MIRANDA
And mine, with my heart in't . . .

They lean toward each other, their lips barely touching.
MIRANDA pulls away.

MIRANDA (CONT'D)
And now farewell. Till half an hour hence.

FERDINAND
>A thousand thousand!

MIRANDA runs ahead while FERDINAND returns to his task.

EXT. IRONWOOD FOREST - AFTERNOON

The KING and his followers make their way through the dense forest.

It is a labyrinth, the trees seeming to subtly move positions.

ALONSO is obsessed with the search for his son.

GONZALO
Had I plantation of this isle, my lord—and
were the king on't, what would I do?

SEBASTIAN
'Scape being drunk for want of wine.

GONZALO
No occupation; all men idle, all;
And women too, but innocent and pure;
No sovereignty.

SEBASTIAN
　　Yet he would be king on't.

ANTONIO
The latter end of his commonwealth forgets
the beginning.

GONZALO
Nature should bring forth,
Of its own kind, all foison, all abundance,
To feed my innocent people.

SEBASTIAN
No marrying 'mong his subjects?

ANTONIO
None, man, all idle—whores and knaves.

GONZALO
I would with such perfection govern, sir,
T'excel the Golden Age.

SEBASTIAN
(loudly)
　　God save His Majesty!

ANTONIO
(loudly)
　　Long live Gonzalo!

GONZALO
　　And—do you mark me, sir?

ALONSO stops suddenly, exasperated with all the talk.

ALONSO
Prithee, no more. Thou dost talk nothing to me.

GONZALO
I do well believe Your Highness; and did
it to minister occasion to these gentlemen,
who are of such sensible and nimble lungs
that they always use to laugh at nothing.

ANTONIO
'Twas you we laughed at.

GONZALO
Who in this kind of merry fooling am
nothing to you; so you may continue and
laugh at nothing still.

ANTONIO
What a blow was there given!

ARIEL darts between the trees, invisible to the court.

SEBASTIAN
Nay, good my lord, be not angry.

GONZALO
No, I warrant you; I will not adventure my
discretion so weakly. Will you laugh me asleep?
For I am very heavy.

ANTONIO
Go sleep, and hear us.

GONZALO lays his cloak on the ground and very quickly
falls asleep.

ALONSO
What, so soon asleep? I wish mine eyes
Would, with themselves, shut up my thoughts.
I find They are inclined to do so.

SEBASTIAN
(offering his cape as a blanket)
　　Please you, sir,
Do not omit the heavy offer of it.
It seldom visits sorrow; when it doth,
It is a comforter.

ANTONIO

    We two, my lord,
Will guard your person while you take your rest,
And watch your safety.

ALONSO

    Thank you. Wondrous heavy.

ALONSO *falls sleeps.*

SEBASTIAN

What a strange drowsiness possesses them!

ANTONIO

It is the quality o' th' climate.

SEBASTIAN

Why doth it not then our eyelids sink?
I find not myself disposed to sleep.

ANTONIO

    Nor I: my spirits are nimble.
They fell together, as by consent.

They dropp'd, as by a thunder-stroke. What might,
Worthy Sebastian— O, what might?— No more!
And yet methinks I see it in thy face,
What thou shouldst be. Th' occasion speaks thee, and
My strong imagination sees a crown
Dropping upon thy head.

SEBASTIAN

    What? Art thou waking?

ANTONIO

    Do you not hear me speak?

SEBASTIAN

    I do; and surely
It is a sleepy language and thou speak'st
Out of thy sleep. What is it thou didst say?
This is a strange repose, to be asleep
With eyes wide open; standing, speaking, moving,
And yet so fast asleep.

ANTONIO
      Noble Sebastian,
Thou let'st thy fortune sleep—die, rather; wink'st
Whiles thou art waking.

SEBASTIAN
      Thou dost snore distinctly;
There's meaning in thy snores.

ANTONIO
I am more serious than my custom. You
Must be so too, if heed me; which to do
Trebles thee o'er.

SEBASTIAN
      Well, I am standing water.

ANTONIO
I'll teach you how to flow.

SEBASTIAN
      Do so. To ebb
Hereditary sloth instructs me.

ANTONIO
      Thus, sir.
Although this lord hath here almost persuaded
the King his son's alive,
'Tis as impossible that he's undrown'd
As he that sleeps here swims.

SEBASTIAN
      I have no hope
That he's undrown'd.

ANTONIO
      O, out of that no hope
What great hope have you! no hope that way is
Another way so high a hope that even

Ambition cannot pierce a wink beyond,
But doubt discovery there. Will you grant with me
That Ferdinand is drown'd?

SEBASTIAN
    He's gone.

ANTONIO
    Then, tell me,
Who's the next heir of Naples?

SEBASTIAN
    Claribel.

ANTONIO
She that is Queen of Tunis; she that dwells
Ten leagues beyond man's life; she that from whom
We all were sea-swallow'd, though some cast again,
And, by that destiny, to perform an act
Whereof what's past is prologue, what to come
In yours and my discharge.

SEBASTIAN
    What stuff is this? How say you?

ANTONIO
    Say, this were death
That now hath seized them, why, they were no worse
Than now they are. There be that can rule Naples
As well as he that sleeps. O, that you bore
The mind that I do! What a sleep were this
For your advancement! Do you understand me?

SEBASTIAN
Methinks I do.

ANTONIO
    And how does your content
Tender your own good fortune?

SEBASTIAN
    I remember
You did supplant your sister Prospera.

ANTONIO
    True.
And look how well my garments sit upon me.
        My sister's servants
Were then my fellows; now they are my men.

SEBASTIAN
But, for your conscience—

ANTONIO
Ay, sir; where lies that? Twenty consciences,
That stand 'twixt me and Milan, candied be they
And melt, ere they molest! Here lies your brother,
No better than the earth he lies upon—
If he were that which now he's like, that's dead—
Whom I, with this obedient steel (three inches of it)
Can lay to bed forever; whiles you, doing thus,
To this ancient morsel, this Sir Prudence, who
Should not upbraid our course.

SEBASTIAN
        Thy case, dear friend,
Shall be my precedent. As thou got'st Milan,
I'll come by Naples. Draw thy sword. One stroke
Shall free thee from the tribute which thou payest,
And I the King shall love thee.

ANTONIO
        Draw together;
And when I rear my hand, do you the like,
To fall it on Gonzalo.

They draw their swords, but their actions are suddenly slowed down
with the appearance of ARIEL. Like a hummingbird buzzing, his sonic
vibrations whirl in the ear of GONZALO.

ARIEL
(whispers)
While you here do snoring lie,
Open-eyed conspiracy
His time doth take. If of life you keep a care,
Shake off slumber, and beware.
Awake, awake!

GONZALO
(wakes, startled)
        Now, good angels
Preserve the King.

ALONSO
(awakes)
Why, how now? Why are you drawn?
Wherefore this ghastly looking?

GONZALO
 What's the matter?

SEBASTIAN and ANTONIO, caught in the act of attempted murder, now try to cover for their actions.

SEBASTIAN
Whiles we stood here securing your repose,
Even now, we heard a hollow burst of bellowing
Like bulls, or rather lions. Did't not wake you?
It struck mine ear most terribly.

ALONSO
 I heard nothing.

ANTONIO
O, 'twas a din to fright a monster's ear,

To make an earthquake!

ALONSO
 Heard you this, Gonzalo?

GONZALO
Upon mine honor, sir, I heard a humming,
Which did awake me. As mine eyes open'd,
I saw their weapons drawn.
'Tis best we stand upon our guard,
Or that we quit this place. Let's draw our weapons.

ALONSO
Lead off this ground, and let's make further search
For my poor son. Lead away.

The court resumes their journey through the woods.

ARIEL
Now Prospera shall know what I have done.
So, King, go safely on to seek thy son.

EXT. THICK BRAMBLE FOREST - AFTERNOON

CALIBAN, STEPHANO, and TRINCULO, totally juiced, stumble through a thicket of gnarled branches.

> **STEPHANO**
> Tell not me! When the butt is out, we will
> drink water; not a drop before. Therefore bear up,
> and board 'em. Servant-monster, drink to me.

> **TRINCULO**
> Servant-monster? The folly of this island!
> They say there's but five upon this isle:
> we are three of them. If th' other two be
> brained like us, the state totters.

> **STEPHANO**
> Mooncalf, speak once in thy life, if thou beest
> a good mooncalf.

> **CALIBAN**
> How does thy honor? Let me lick thy shoe.
> I'll not serve him; he's not valiant.

> **TRINCULO**
> Thou liest, most ignorant monster; Why, thou
> deboshed fish thou. Wilt thou tell a monstrous
> lie, being but half a fish and half a monster?

> **CALIBAN**
> Lo, how he mocks me! Wilt thou let him, my lord?

> **TRINCULO**
> "Lord" quoth he! That a monster should be such a natural!

> **CALIBAN**
> Lo, lo, again! bite him to death, I prithee.

> **STEPHANO**
> Trinculo, keep a good tongue in your head.
> If you prove a mutineer—the next tree!
> The poor monster's my subject and he shall not suffer indignity.

> **CALIBAN**
> I thank my noble lord. Wilt thou be pleased to
> hearken once again to the suit I made to thee?

> **STEPHANO**
> Marry, will I. Kneel and repeat it; I will stand,
> and so shall Trinculo.

TRINCULO, pissed at the favor CALIBAN is receiving from STEPHANO, glumly rises.

> **CALIBAN**
> As I told thee before, I am subject to a tyrant,
> A sorceress, that by her cunning hath
> Cheated me of the island.

ARIEL, invisible to the three conspirators, suddenly appears from behind TRINCULO, who is not paying much attention to the story of CALIBAN.

> **ARIEL**
> Thou liest.

CALIBAN, thinking it was TRINCULO who accused him, turns on the unsuspecting fool.

> **CALIBAN**
> Thou liest, thou jesting monkey, thou.
> I do not lie.

> **STEPHANO**
> Trinculo, if you trouble him any more in's tale, by this hand,
> I will supplant some of your teeth.

TRINCULO
Why, I said nothing.

STEPHANO
Mum, then, and no more. Proceed.

CALIBAN
I say, by sorcery she got this isle;
From me she got it. If thy greatness will
Revenge it on her,
Thou shalt be lord of it and I'll serve thee.

STEPHANO
How now shall this be compassed? Canst thou bring
me to the party?

CALIBAN
Yea, yea, my lord! I'll yield her thee asleep,
Where thou mayst knock a nail into her head.

ARIEL
(again pretending to be TRINCULO)
Thou liest; thou canst not.

CALIBAN
What a pied ninny's this! Thou scurvy patch!
I do beseech thy greatness, give him blows
And take his bottle from him.

TRINCULO
Why, what did I? I did nothing. I'll go farther off.

STEPHANO
Didst thou not say he lied?

ARIEL
Thou liest.

STEPHANO
Do I so? Take thou that.
(strikes TRINCULO)
As you like this, give me the lie another time.

TRINCULO
I did not give the lie. Out o' your wits and bearing too? A pox o'
your bottle! And the devil take your fingers!

CALIBAN
Ha, ha, ha!

STEPHANO
Now, forward with your tale.
(to TRINCULO)
Prithee, stand farther off. Come, proceed.

CALIBAN
Why, as I told thee, 'tis a custom with her,
I' th' (late) afternoon to sleep: there thou mayst brain her,
Having first seized her books, or with a log
Batter her skull, or paunch her with a stake,
Or cut her weasand with thy knife. Remember
First to possess her books; for without them
She's but a sot, as I am, nor hath not
One spirit to command: they all do hate her

As rootedly as I. Burn but her books.
And that most deeply to consider is
The beauty of her daughter. Of women
I've seen but these and Sycorax my dam.
But she as far surpasseth Sycorax
As great'st does least.

STEPHANO
Is it so brave a lass?

CALIBAN
Ay, lord; she will become thy bed, I warrant.
And bring thee forth brave brood.

STEPHANO
Monster, I will kill this witch: her daughter
and I will be King and Queen—and Trinculo and

116

thyself shall be viceroys. Dost thou like the
plot, Trinculo?

TRINCULO
(sullenly)
Excellent.

STEPHANO
Give me thy hand. I am sorry I beat thee.

CALIBAN
Within this half hour will she be asleep.
Wilt thou destroy her then?

STEPHANO
Ay, on mine honor.

ARIEL
(to himself)
This will I tell my master.

CALIBAN
Thou makest me merry; I am full of pleasure.

STEPHANO
Come on, Trinculo, let us sing.
(sings)
Flout 'em and scout 'em
And scout 'em and flout 'em
  Thought is free.

EXT. SISAL FOREST - DAY

TRINCULO joins in on the singing.

TRINCULO
Grog 'em then flog 'em
And flog 'em and grog 'em

STEPHANO AND TRINCULO
Thought is free

Suddenly loud, unearthly music mimics the sound and rhythm of their song. It startles and frightens STEPHANO and TRINCULO.

STEPHANO
What is this same? If thou beest a man, show thyself.

TRINCULO
O, forgive me my sins!

STEPHANO
Mercy upon us!

CALIBAN
Art thou afeard?

STEPHANO
No, monster, not I.

CALIBAN
Be not afeard; the isle is full of noises,
Sounds and sweet airs, that give delight and hurt not.
Sometimes a thousand twangling instruments
Will hum about mine ears, and sometime voices
That, if I then had waked after long sleep,
Will make me sleep again; and then, in dreaming,
The clouds methought would open and show riches
Ready to drop upon me that, when I waked,
I cried to dream again.

STEPHANO
(aside to TRINCULO)
This will prove a brave kingdom to me,
where I shall have my music for nothing.

CALIBAN
When Prospera is destroyed.

INT. PROSPERA'S LAB - LATE AFTERNOON

PROSPERA works at her "alchemical laboratory" in the cave below the earth.

Her books are scattered everywhere.

She works with a fierce intensity, collecting and distilling the moon's beams in a "da Vinci"-like glass and iron apparatus.

EXT. FOREST OPENING ONTO BLACK VOLCANIC LANDSCAPE - LATE AFTERNOON/ SOLAR ECLIPSE

ALONSO, SEBASTIAN, ANTONIO, and GONZALO stumble through the dark forest and come into an open clearing.

They are exhausted and their tempers are worn thin.

GONZALO
By'r lakin, I can go no further, sir.
I needs must rest me.

ALONSO
　　Old lord, I cannot blame thee,
Who am myself attach'd with weariness.
Sit down, and rest. He is drown'd
Whom thus we stray to find; and the sea mocks
Our frustrate search on land.
Well, let him go.

ANTONIO
(aside to SEBASTIAN)
I am right glad that he's so out of hope.

SEBASTIAN
(aside to ANTONIO)
The next advantage will we take thoroughly.

ANTONIO
(aside to SEBASTIAN)
Let it be tonight.

Suddenly, a SOLAR ECLIPSE turns day into night.

Solemn and strange music accompanies the image of a lavish banquet that appears to hover, magically, in the middle of the threatening landscape.

Through time-lapse animation, volcanic stepping-stones appear and become a smooth footpath to the banquet table.

[From this point on, until PROSPERA restores the natural order of daylight, the landscapes will be illuminated with light from the "solar eclipse," which causes them to be surreal.]

They walk down the path to the banquet table, which is laden with exotic steaming platters of every manner of food.

ALONSO
What harmony is this? My good friends, hark!

GONZALO
Marvellous sweet music!

ALONSO
Give us kind keepers, heavens!

SEBASTIAN
A living drollery. Now I will believe
That there are unicorns.

GONZALO
    If in Naples
I should report this now, would they believe me?

SEBASTIAN
We have stomachs. Will't please you taste of what is here?

ALONSO
Not I.

GONZALO
Faith, sir, you need not fear.

ALONSO
    I will stand to and feed;
Although my last: no matter, since I feel
The best is past. Brother, my lord the duke,
Stand to and do as we.

As they commence to partake . . .

CUT TO: INT. PROSPERA'S LAB - SAME

PROSPERA drops a raven's feather into a vial of bubbling liquid.

The glass explodes into . . .

CUT TO: EXT. BLACK VOLCANIC LANDSCAPE - DARK FROM THE ECLIPSE

Thunder and lightning.

ARIEL appears as a GIANT HARPY that divides into hundreds of blackbirds/harpies, their wings madly flapping.

They attack the banquet table, the KING, ANTONIO, and SEBASTIAN.

The banquet vanishes in a whirlwind of ash and black feathers.

A roaring wind continues.

ARIEL, the harpy, its breasts, face, and talons covered in black, oozing oil, chants in a distorted and terrifying voice. With giant wings outstretched, this creature sits, perched on a volcanic mound of shattered glass in the center of the banquet table.

The KING, ANTONIO, and SEBASTIAN stand frozen, terrorized.

> ARIEL
> You are three men of sin, whom destiny
> Hath caused to belch up you; and on this island
> Where man doth not inhabit—you 'mongst men
> Being most unfit to live—I have made you mad.

ANTONIO, ALONSO, and SEBASTIAN draw their swords, thrashing away at the attacking harpies.

> ARIEL MULTIPLIED (CONT'D)
> You fools! I and my fellows
> Are ministers of Fate: the elements,
> Of whom your swords are temper'd, may as well
> Wound the loud winds, as diminish
> One dowle that's in my plume. But remember—
> For that's my business to you—that you three
> From Milan did supplant good Prospera;
> Her and her innocent child; for which foul deed
> The powers, delaying, not forgetting, have
> Incensed the seas and shores, yea, all the creatures,
> Against your peace. Thee of thy son, Alonso,
> They have bereft; and do pronounce by me
> Lingering perdition shall step by step attend
> You and your ways.

ARIEL and all the harpies vanish with the thunder.

INT. PROSPERA'S LAB - SAME

> PROSPERA
> Bravely the figure of this harpy hast thou
> Perform'd, my Ariel. My high charms work
> And these mine enemies are all knit up
> In their distractions; they now are in my pow'r.

You are three men of sin

I have made you mad!

EXT. BLACK VOLCANIC LANDSCAPE - ECLIPSE

The banquet evaporated, GONZALO stares at his KING, who stands over an oozing puddle of black oil.

> **GONZALO**
> I' the name of something holy, sir, why stand you
> In this strange stare?

> **ALONSO**
>   O, it is monstrous, monstrous!
> Methought the billows spoke and told me of it;
> The winds did sing it to me; and the thunder,
> That deep and dreadful organ pipe, pronounced
> The name of Prospera: it did bass my trespass.
> Therefore my son i' th' ooze is bedded, and
> I'll seek him deeper than e'er plummet sounded
> And with him there lie mudded.

He wanders off, leaving GONZALO mystified.

SEBASTIAN and ANTONIO wildly strike at the air with their swords.

> **SEBASTIAN**
>   But one fiend at a time,

I'll fight their legions o'er.

> **ANTONIO**
>   I'll be thy second.

They disappear into the distance, chasing and being chased by an invisible enemy.

> **GONZALO**
> All three of them are desperate: their great guilt,
> Like poison given to work a great time after,
> Now 'gins to bite the spirits.
> I shall follow them swiftly
> And hinder them from what this ecstasy
> May now provoke them to.

He chases after the KING and company.

EXT. HIGH PROMONTORY OVERLOOKING THE OCEAN/SOLAR ECLIPSE

FERDINAND and PROSPERA stand a good distance apart, ceremoniously facing each other.

MIRANDA stands before her mother, PROSPERA'S hands clasping her shoulders.

As she speaks, PROSPERA slowly turns her daughter to face FERDINAND.

> **PROSPERA**
> If I have too austerely punish'd you,
> Your compensation makes amends, for I
> Have given you here a third of mine own life,
> Or that for which I live; all thy vexations
> Were but my trials of thy love and thou
> Hast strangely stood the test. O Ferdinand,
> Do not smile at me that I boast of her,
> For thou shalt find she will outstrip all praise
> And make it halt behind her.

> **FERDINAND**
>   I do believe it against an oracle.

> **PROSPERA**
> Then, as my gift and thine own acquisition
> Worthily purchased, take my daughter.

She releases MIRANDA, who slowly moves to FERDINAND.

PROSPERA (CONT'D)
        But
If thou dost break her virgin-knot before
All sanctimonious ceremonies,
No sweet aspersion shall the heavens let fall
To make this contract grow.

FERDINAND
        As I hope for quiet days, fair issue and long life,
the strongest temptation
Shall never melt
Mine honor into lust.

PROSPERA
        Fairly spoke.

Sit then and talk with her; she is thine own.

They grab each other's hands and sit, close together, on the high prom-ontory, facing the sea and the dark sky. PROSPERA leaves the two lovers alone.

EXT. MANGROVE SWAMP - DARK FROM THE ECLIPSE

STEPHANO and TRINCULO, miserable and wet, trudge through the swamp after CALIBAN.

STEPHANO
Monster, your fairy, which you say is a harmless fairy, has done little better than played the Jack with us.

TRINCULO
Monster, I do smell all horse-piss, at which
my nose is in great indignation.

STEPHANO
So is mine. Do you hear, monster?

CALIBAN
Good my lord, give me thy favor still.

TRINCULO
Ay, but to lose our bottles in the pool—

STEPHANO
There is not only disgrace and dishonor in

that, monster, but an infinite loss.

TRINCULO
That's more to me than my wetting. Yet this is
your harmless fairy, monster.

He slips on the muddy bank and falls ass backward into the pool.
From under the water leap a dozen startled frogs that curiously
resemble ARIEL.

PROSPERA (O.C.)
What, Ariel!

**EXT. HIGH PROMONTORY OVERLOOKING
THE OCEAN – SOLAR ECLIPSE**

PROSPERA
My industrious servant, Ariel!

ARIEL flies to her side.

ARIEL
What would my potent master? Here I am.

PROSPERA
   Go bring the rabble,
O'er whom I give thee pow'r, here to this place.
Incite them to quick motion; for I must
Bestow upon the eyes of this young couple
Some vanity of mine art: it is my promise,
And they expect it from me.

ARIEL
   Presently?

PROSPERA
Ay, with a twink.

ARIEL
Before you can say "Come" and "Go!"
Do you love me, master? No?

PROSPERA
Dearly my delicate Ariel.

ARIEL disappears.

CUT TO:

On another part of the promontory, FERDINAND and MIRANDA are
now sitting quite close to one another on the soft grass. He turns to her
and begins to whisper a love song into her ear.

FERDINAND
O mistress mine, where are you roaming?
Oh stay and hear! Your true love's coming
   That can sing both high and low;
Trip no further, pretty sweeting,
Journeys end in Lover's meeting—
   Every wise man's son doth know.

What is love? 'tis not hereafter;
Present mirth hath present laughter;
    What's to come is still unsure;
In delay there lies no plenty—
Then come kiss me, Sweet-and-twenty,
    Youth's a stuff will not endure.

During the song, his hands and hers slowly begin a cautious tour of each other's bodies until they are entwined and lost in each other's embrace.

PROSPERA turns to find the two young lovers passionately kissing.

PROSPERA
Look thou be true. Do not give dalliance
Too much the rein; the strongest oaths are straw
To the fire i' th' blood.

The two lovers bolt upright at being caught.

FERDINAND
I warrant you madam.
The white cold virgin snow upon my heart
Abates the ardor of my liver.

PROSPERA
Well.

PROSPERA, in her cloak and with her staff, calls forth the vision.

PROSPERA
No tongue! All eyes! Be silent.

A thrilling spectacle of sea creatures and constellations dance together and explode like fireworks before the eyes of the young couple, melding sky and ocean in an animated alchemical chart.

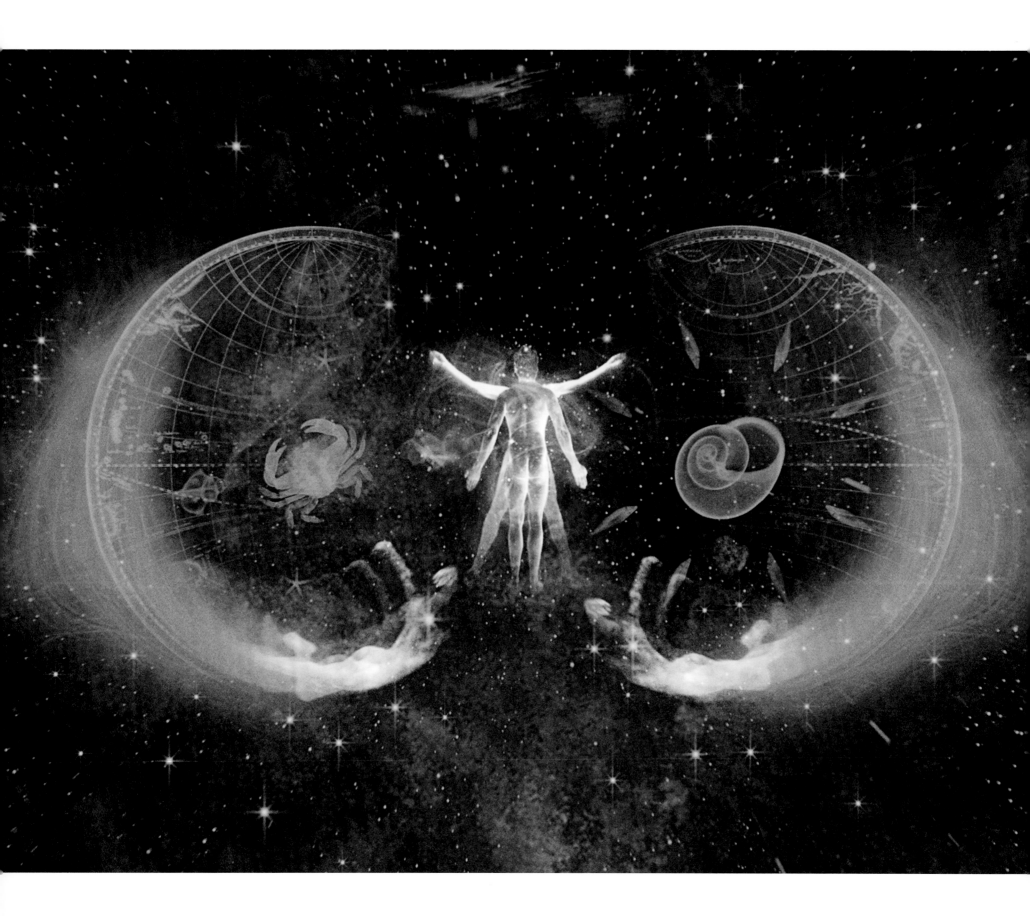

PROSPERA
(aside)
I had forgot that foul conspiracy
Of the beast Caliban and his confederates
Against my life.
(to the spirits in the sky)
Avoid! No more! No more!

The spectacle dissolves with PROSPERA'S command, and the gray, brooding sky returns.

The seas below are rough and dark.

FERDINAND
This is strange. Your mother's in some passion
That works her strongly.

MIRANDA
    Never till this day
Saw I her touch'd with anger so distemper'd.

PROSPERA
You do look, my son, in a moved sort,
As if you were dismay'd: be cheerful, sir.
Our revels now are ended. These our actors,
As I foretold you, were all spirits and
Are melted into air, into thin air;
And, like the baseless fabric of this vision,
The cloud-capp'd towers, the gorgeous palaces,
The solemn temples, the great globe itself,
Yea, all which it inherit, shall dissolve
And, like this insubstantial pageant faded,
Leave not a rack behind. We are such stuff
As dreams are made on, and our little life
Is rounded with a sleep. Sir, I am vex'd.
If you be pleased, retire into my cell
And there repose: a turn or two I'll walk,
To still my beating mind.

FERDINAND AND MIRANDA
We wish your peace.

They rise to follow the path to the cell.

PROSPERA
Come with a thought!
I thank thee, Ariel. Come.

As if out of the forehead of PROSPERA, ARIEL appears.

We are such stuff
As dreams are made on,
and our little life
Is rounded with a sleep.

ARIEL
What's thy pleasure?

PROSPERA
       Spirit,
We must prepare to meet with Caliban.

ARIEL
Ay, my commander.

PROSPERA
Say again, where didst thou leave these varlets?

ARIEL
I told you, ma'am, they were red-hot with drinking.
               I left them
I' the filthy-mantled pool beyond your cell,
There dancing up to the chins, that the foul lake
Outstunk their feet.

PROSPERA
       This was well done, my bird.
The trumpery in my house, go put it out,
For stale to catch these thieves.

ARIEL
       I go, I go.

Off in a flash.

PROSPERA
A devil, a born devil, on whose nature
Nurture can never stick; on whom my pains,
Humanely taken, all, all lost, quite lost!
I will plague them all, even to roaring.

EXT. HIGH CLIFF TRAIL TO THE CELL - DARK

CALIBAN, STEPHANO, and TRINCULO, dripping wet, make their
clumsy way, trying to quietly steal along the high wall.

CALIBAN
Pray you, tread softly. We now are near her cell.

EXT. THE ENTRY DOWN THE WALL OF THE LAVA GARDEN - DARK

> CALIBAN
> Prithee, be quiet. Seest thou here?
> This is the mouth o' the cell. No noise, and enter.

> STEPHANO
> Give me thy hand. I do begin to have bloody thoughts.

They move through the inner garden.

TRINCULO tries to pick some of the succulent fruit from the trees and is smacked on the head by STEPHANO.

CALIBAN shushes the two.

They come to the entry of the cave.

Before them is stretched a magical clothesline from which hangs all manner of rich and gaudy garments, mostly feminine. It hangs just in front of a circular pool of water that is the dwelling's cistern.

> TRINCULO
> O King Stephano! O worthy Stephano! Look what a wardrobe here is for thee!

> CALIBAN
> Let it alone, thou fool! It is but trash.

> TRINCULO
> O, ho, monster! We know what belongs to a frippery.

He grabs a royal robe and dramatically twirls it over his shoulders.

> **TRINCULO (CONT'D)**
> O King Stephano!

> **STEPHANO**
> Put off that gown, Trinculo! By this hand, I'll have that gown.

> **TRINCULO**
> *(throwing him the robe)*
> Thy Grace shall have it.

The two fools grab at the fancy clothes, trying them on, holding them up to each other's bodies and generally having a ball.

> **CALIBAN**
> What do you mean to dote thus on such luggage?
> Let's alone and do the murder first.

> **STEPHANO**
> Be you quiet, monster.

STEPHANO addresses the clothesline.

> **STEPHANO (CONT'D)**
> Mistress line, is not this my jerkin?

He jerks a jacket off the line, howling at his clever punning.

> **TRINCULO**
> Do, do! We steal by line and level, and't like your Grace.

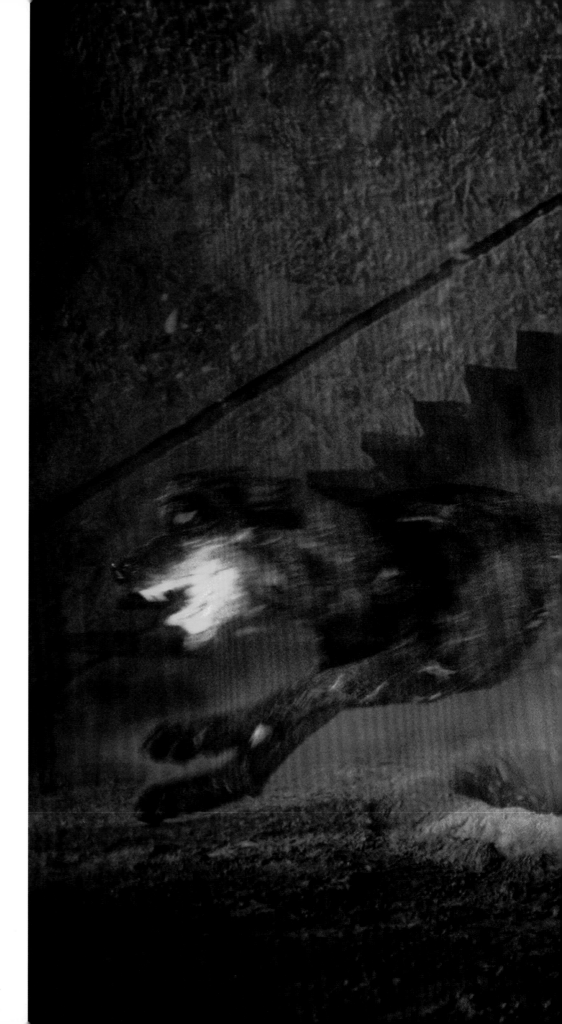

STEPHANO
I thank thee for that jest. Here's a garment for't.
Wit shall not go unrewarded while I am king of
this country.

TRINCULO
Monster, come, put some lime upon your fingers,
And away with the rest.

CALIBAN
I will have none on't. We shall lose our time,
And all be turned to barnacles.

STEPHANO
Monster, lay-to your fingers, or I'll turn you out of my
Kingdom. Go to, carry this.

STEPHANO and TRINCULO start ripping the rest of the clothes off the
line and throwing them into the arms of a very distressed CALIBAN.

TRINCULO
And this.

STEPHANO
Ay, and this.

From the pool of water, that has suddenly transformed into bubbling
fire and lava, a pack of growling and barking dogs emerges to chase away
the thieves.

Part black beast and part fire, these dogs nip at the backsides and heels
of the three fools, driving them up and out of PROSPERA'S grounds.
Once the lava dogs have emerged out of the lava field, ARIEL'S face
is revealed, composed of bubbling lava, laughing and screaming with
delight and ferocity.

PROSPERA, from high up on the cell's walls, yells to the dogs.

PROSPERA
Hey, mountain, hey!

ARIEL
Silver! There it goes, Silver!

PROSPERA
Fury, fury! There, tyrant, there! Hark! Hark!

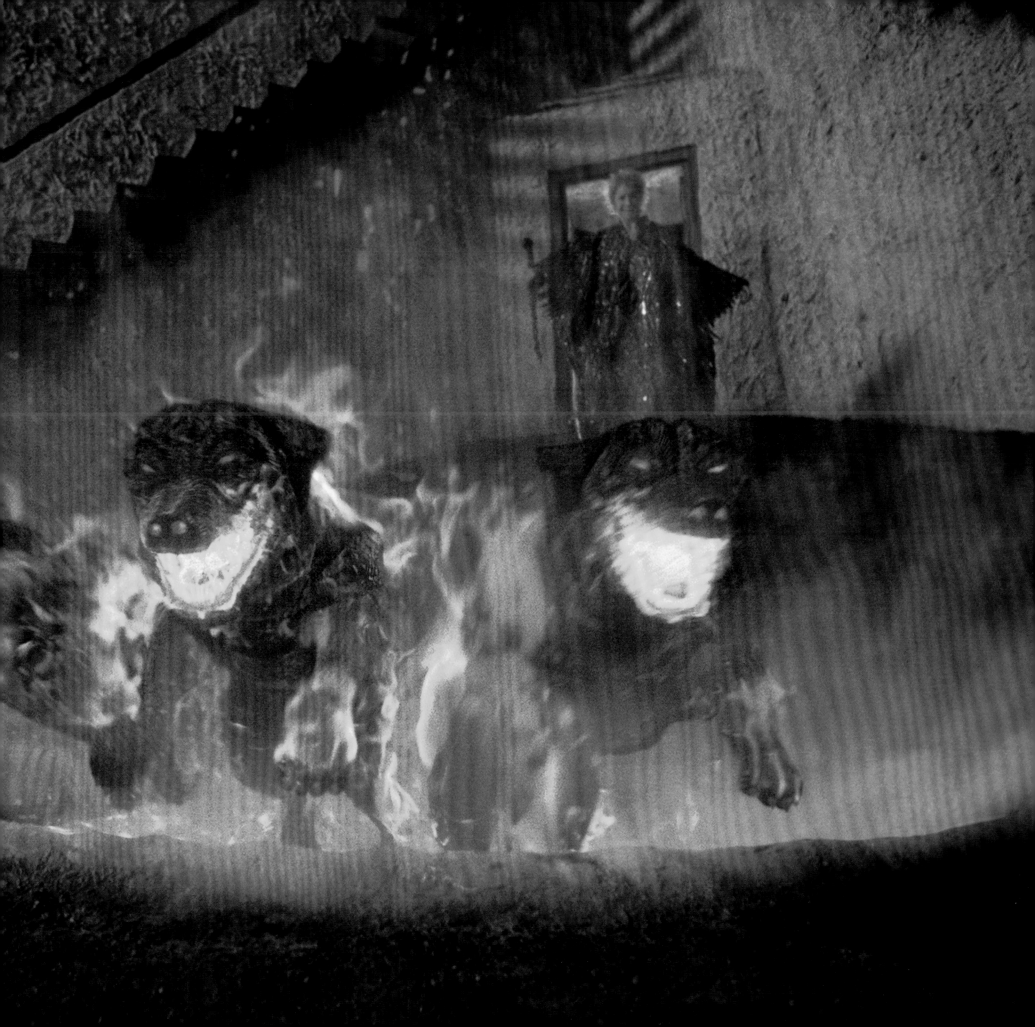

EXT. LAVA HILL - DARK

The molten lava in the form of rabid dogs continues to chase them down the steep black hill.

Sparks flying, the barking and growling beasts show no mercy.

> ARIEL (O.C.)
> Hark, they roar!

EXT. BLACK VOLCANIC HILL - DARK

PROSPERA stands on the top of her stairs etched with fire behind her and molten lava flowing down the ridges and radiating out. The atmosphere is charged with heat and undulation. The sky is blood red.

> PROSPERA
> *(yelling)*
> Let them be hunted soundly!

She turns to speak to herself and to ARIEL.

> At this hour
> Lie at my mercy all mine enemies.
> Now does my project gather to a head.
> Shortly shall all my labors end, and thou
> Shalt have the air at freedom.

EXT. BLACK VOLCANIC LANDSCAPE - DARK

The KING and GONZALO sit underneath the sole green tree in this harsh landscape, their heads in their hands.

A distressed GONZALO looks up and watches as SEBASTIAN and ANTONIO move off into the distance, still slashing away hysterically at invisible demons.

> PROSPERA (O.C.)
> Say, my spirit,
> How fares the King and's followers?

ARIEL (O.C.)
　　Confined together
In the same fashion as you gave in charge,
Just as you left them—all prisoners, ma'am.
The King, his brother and yours, abide all three distracted,
　　　　but chiefly,
Him that you term'd, ma'am, "The good old lord Gonzalo" . . .

EXT. PROSPERA'S CELL - THE LIBRARY - DARK

On PROSPERA'S face as ARIEL continues.

ARIEL (CONT'D)
. . . His tears run down his beard, like winter's drops
From eaves of reeds. Your charm so strongly works 'em
That if you now beheld them, your affections
Would become tender.

PROSPERA
　　Dost thou think so, spirit?

ARIEL
Mine would, master, were I human.

PROSPERA
　　And mine shall.
Hast thou, which art but air, a touch, a feeling
Of their afflictions, and shall not myself,
One of their kind, be kindlier moved than thou art?
Though with their high wrongs I am struck to th' quick,
Yet with my nobler reason 'gainst my fury
Do I take part. The rarer action is
In virtue than in vengeance. They being penitent,
The sole drift of my purpose doth extend
Not a frown further. Go, release them, Ariel.
My charms I'll break, their senses I'll restore,
And they shall be themselves.

ARIEL
　　I'll fetch them, ma'am.

EXT. GARDEN OF THE GODS - DARK TO SUNSET

PROSPERA draws a magic circle in the red earth floor with her staff.

The circle burns.

As she draws, the moon moves away from the sun and daylight is restored.

The sun is low and red in the sky, causing the land to appear even redder.

As she turns, the landscape moves around her, at first spinning slowly, then faster and faster until it is a blurred swirl. The fire and smoky skies are moving in contrary motion and at a different speed than the landscape, as she describes the violent and supernatural acts that she has conjured.

> **PROSPERA**
> Ye elves of hills, brooks, standing lakes and groves,
> And ye that on the sands with printless foot
> Do chase the ebbing Neptune and do fly him
> When he comes back; you demi-puppets that
> By moonshine do the green sour ringlets make,
> Whereof the ewe not bites; and you whose pastime
> Is to make midnight mushrooms, that rejoice
> To hear the solemn curfew; by whose aid
> (Weak masters though ye be) I have bedimm'd
> The noontide sun, call'd forth the mutinous winds,

And 'twixt the green sea and the azured vault
Set roaring war; to the dread rattling thunder
Have I given fire and rifted Jove's stout oak
With his own bolt; the strong-based promontory
Have I made shake and by the spurs pluck'd up
The pine and cedar; graves at my command
Have waked their sleepers, oped, and let 'em forth
By my so potent art.

She comes to a sudden standstill. The fire retreats into the earth. The dizzying skies stop churning.

Utterly internal.

> PROSPERA (CONT'D)
> But this rough magic
> I here abjure; and, when I have required
> Some heavenly music (which even now I do)
> To work mine end upon their senses that
> This airy charm is for, I'll break my staff,
> Bury it certain fathoms in the earth,
> And deeper than did ever plummet sound
> I'll drown my book.

She looks up to see ARIEL leading the entranced ANTONIO, ALONSO, GONZALO, and SEBASTIAN down the red hills. They are compelled into the circle that PROSPERA has made, and there stand frozen, charmed; while PROSPERA, moving amongst them, speaks.

> PROSPERA (CONT'D)
>   There stand,
> For you are spell-stopp'd.
>   O good Gonzalo,
> My true preserver, and a loyal sir
> To him you follow'st, I will pay thy graces
> Home both in word and deed. Most cruelly
> Didst thou, Alonso, use me and my daughter.
> Thy brother was a furtherer in the act.
> Thou art pinched for't now, Sebastian. Flesh and blood,
> You, brother mine, that entertain'd ambition,
> Expell'd remorse and nature; who, with Sebastian,
> Would here have killed your king, I do forgive thee,
> Unnatural though thou art.

She exits the circle.

>   Their understanding
> Begins to swell.

> Ariel,
> Fetch me the skirt and bodice in my cell.
> I will discase me, and myself present
> As I was sometime Milan. Quickly, spirit!
> Thou shalt ere long be free.

ARIEL goes and returns in a flash.

He helps to attire her.

The corset PROSPERA has not worn for these past twelve years is pulled tight around her waist and chest, and laced from the back.

Each tug of the cord by ARIEL'S nimble fingers is a reminder of where she came from and where she will be going.

A faint smile betrays the sacrifice.

> PROSPERA (CONT'D)
> O I shall miss thee Ariel,
> But yet thou shalt have freedom; so, so, so.

She turns her attention to the four NOBLES who have regained their senses. Shocked, they stare at the vision of PROSPERA, who stands before them.

PROSPERA (CONT'D)
Behold the wrongèd Duchess of Milan—
Prospera. I bid a hearty welcome.

She moves into the circle.

ALONSO
      Whe'r thou be'st she or no,
Or some enchanted trifle to abuse me,
         I not know: thy pulse
Beats as of flesh and blood; and, since I saw thee,
Th' affliction of my mind amends, with which,
I fear, a madness held me. This must crave
(And if this be at all) a most strange story.
Thy dukedom I resign and do entreat
Thou pardon me my wrongs. But how should Prospera
Be living and be here?

PROSPERA
(turns to GONZALO)
      First, noble friend,
Let me embrace thine age, whose honor cannot
Be measured or confined.

GONZALO
      Whether this be
Or be not, I'll not swear.

PROSPERA
      You do yet taste
Some subtleties o' the isle, that will not let you
Believe things certain. Welcome, my friends all.
(turning to SEBASTIAN and ANTONIO)
But you, my brace of lords, were I so minded,
I here could pluck his Highness' frown upon you
And justify you traitors: at this time
I will tell no tales.

SEBASTIAN
(aside)
The devil speaks in her.

PROSPERA
      No.
(to ANTONIO)
For you, most wicked sir, whom to call brother
Would even infect my mouth, I do forgive
Thy rankest fault—all of them; and require

My dukedom of thee, which perforce, I know,
Thou must restore.

ALONSO
    If thou beest Prospera,
Give us particulars of thy preservation;
How thou hast met us here, who three hours since
Were wracked upon this shore; where I have lost
My dear son Ferdinand.

PROSPERA
    I am woe for't, sir, for I have lost my daughter.

ALONSO
    A daughter? When did you lose your daughter?

PROSPERA
In this last tempest. But, howsoe'er you have
Been justled from your senses, know for certain
That I am Prospera.

EXT./INT. PROSPERA'S CELL, THE HIGH - WALLED GARDEN - DUSK

> PROSPERA (CONT'D)
> Welcome, sir;
> This cell's my court.

ALONSO and the others enter the cell, marvelling at the surreal garden, high walls, and steep stairs.

PROSPERA motions for the KING to mount the hill to a high door.

> PROSPERA (CONT'D)
> Pray you, look in.

At the top he looks through the door and finds FERDINAND and MIRANDA playing chess.

They are oblivious to the arrival of PROSPERA and the KING.

INT. LIBRARY - DUSK

The room is filled with PROSPERA'S books. In the center of the small space the young lovers play chess with handmade pieces made of coral and lava rock.

> MIRANDA
> Sweet lord, you play me false.

> FERDINAND
> No, my dear'st love, I would not for the world.

> MIRANDA
> Yes, for a score of kingdoms you should wrangle,
> And I would call it, fair play.

> ALONSO
> *(from the doorway)*
> If this prove

A vision of the island, one dear son
Shall I twice lose.

SEBASTIAN has also climbed the steep incline and looks through the doorway.

SEBASTIAN
A most high miracle!

FERDINAND
(astounded to see his father alive)
Though the seas threaten, they are merciful.
I have cursed them without cause.

He kneels at the foot of his father.

ALONSO
Now all the blessings
Of a glad father compass thee about!
Arise, and say how thou camest here.

MIRANDA stands at the door of the library and gazes down on the rest of the court.

MIRANDA
O, wonder!
How many goodly creatures are there here!
How beauteous mankind is! O brave new world,
That has such people in't!

PROSPERA
'Tis new to thee.

ALONSO
What is this maid with whom thou wast at play?
Is she the goddess that hath sever'd us
And brought us thus together?

FERDINAND
    Sir, she is mortal;
But by immortal providence she's mine.
I chose her when I could not ask my father
For his advice, nor thought I had one.

ALONSO
Give me your hands.

ALONSO takes the hands of FERDINAND and MIRANDA between his own in a formal gesture of acceptance of their union.

GONZALO
    Be it so! Amen!

From deep in the half-moon pool ARIEL appears to PROSPERA.

ARIEL
    Was't well done?

PROSPERA
(aside to ARIEL)
Bravely, my diligence. Set Caliban and his confederates free.
Untie the spell.

EXT. CLIFF PATH TO PROSPERA'S CELL - DUSK

ARIEL, as a cloud of stinging bees, drives CALIBAN, STEPHANO, and TRINCULO, still decked out in their stolen ladies' apparel, up the steep incline.

STEPHANO
Every man shift for all the rest.
Coragio, bully-monster, coragio!

The horde of bees will not allow them to run in any other direction but straight up the path to PROSPERA'S cell. TRINCULO and CALIBAN howl in pain, madly trying to shoo away the bees.

O brave new world,
That has such people in't!

EXT./INT. PROSPERA'S CELL AND GARDEN - DUSK

The COURT, PROSPERA, FERDINAND, and MIRANDA are surprised at the raucous and howling sight that hurtles down the steps of the cell. The three clowns are just as surprised at the royal company now before them.

TRINCULO
If these be true spies which I wear in my head, here's a goodly sight.

CALIBAN
O Setebos, these be brave spirits indeed!
How fine my master is! I am afraid
She will chastise me.

SEBASTIAN
            Ha, ha! What things are these, my lord Antonio?
Will money buy 'em?

ANTONIO
            Very like. One of them
Is a plain fish, and no doubt marketable.

PROSPERA
These three have robb'd me,
and have plotted together
To take my life. Two of these fellows you
Must know and own. This thing of darkness I
Acknowledge mine.

CALIBAN
I shall be pinched to death.

ALONSO
Is not this Stephano, my drunken butler?

ANTONIO
And Trinculo is reeling ripe.
How camest thou in this pickle?

TRINCULO
I have been in such a pickle since I saw you last that, I fear me, will never out of my bones.

SEBASTIAN
Why, how now, Stephano!

STEPHANO
O, touch me not! I am not Stephano, but a cramp.

PROSPERA
You'd be king o' the isle, sirrah?

STEPHANO
I should have been a sore one then.

ALONSO
This is a strange thing as e'er I look'd on.
(pointing to CALIBAN)

CALIBAN
What a thrice-double ass
Was I, to take this drunkard for a god
And worship this dull fool!

PROSPERA
    Go to! Away!

CALIBAN does not budge but simply keeps his head bent and his eyes lowered to the earth. PROSPERA, also very still, keeps her eyes glued to CALIBAN.

ALONSO turns to the two thieves.

ALONSO
Hence, and bestow your luggage where you found it.

SEBASTIAN
Or stole it, rather.

STEPHANO and TRINCULO enter the cave cell.

The tension between CALIBAN and PROSPERA is taut and the room feels it. Abruptly PROSPERA, herself, lightens the mood by inviting everyone to her cell.

PROSPERA
Sir, I invite your Highness and your train
To my poor cell, where you shall take your rest
For this one night. And in the morn
I'll bring you to your ship and so to Naples,
Where I have hope to see the nuptial
Of these our dear-beloved solemnizèd.

As she ushers them in, she passes CALIBAN who remains frozen as a rock.

Under her breath she mutters . . .

PROSPERA (CONT'D)
And thence retire me to my Milan, where
Every third thought shall be my grave.

All of the party move into the cave, leaving PROSPERA outside.

She turns to find CALIBAN, still motionless, in the exact same position. Finally he looks up, directly into her eyes. He then looks to her staff, expecting PROSPERA to use it against him. It is almost inconceivable that the punishment and torture do not come.

PROSPERA takes in the full measure of her own responsibility for CALIBAN. There is a silent moment of communion between them. CALIBAN turns, climbs up the steep steps. For a moment he hesitates in the doorway, then exits the courtyard without looking back.

With a sigh, as if the heavy clouds of the tempest had been lifted from her shoulders, PROSPERA whispers to the wind.

PROSPERA
My Ariel, chick,
That is thy charge. Then to the elements be free.

ARIEL falls away from PROSPERA into a never-ending abyss, his translucent form dividing and multiplying into a kaleidoscope of rushing waters until he finally dissolves into the sea.

ARIEL
(singing)
Where the bee sucks, there suck I
In a cowslip's bell I lie
There I couch when owl's do cry
On a bat's back I do fly,
After summer merrily,
Merrily, merrily shall I live now
Under the blossom that hangs on the bough.

EXT. HIGH PROMONTORY OVER LOOKING THE OCEAN - NIGHT

As promised, PROSPERA throws her staff off of the cliff and watches it shatter into millions of pieces on the rocks below.

PROSPERA'S books slowly sink one by one into the deep, black sea as the main credits begin. A haunting female voice sings Prospera's last speech

> *Now my charms are all o'erthrown,*
> *And what strength I have's mine own,*
> *Which is most faint:*
> *Oh release me from my bands*
> *With the help of your good hands:*
> *Gentle breath of yours my sails*
> *Must fill, or else my project fails,*
> *Which was to please.*
> *Now I lack spirits to enforce, art to enchant,*
> *And my ending is despair,*
> *Unless I be relieved by prayer,*
> *Which pierces so that it assaults*
> *Mercy itself and frees all faults.*
> *As you from crimes would pardon'd be,*
> *Let your indulgence set me free.*

Touchstone Pictures presents a Miranda Films, TalkStory Productions, Artemis Films Production,
in Association with Mumbai Mantra Media Limited and Prologue Films

THE TEMPEST

DIRECTED BY	Julie Taymor
SCREENPLAY BY	Julie Taymor
ADAPTED FROM THE PLAY BY	William Shakespeare
PRODUCED BY	Julie Taymor, Robert Chartoff, and Lynn Hendee
PRODUCED BY	Julia Taylor-Stanley and Jason K. Lau
EXECUTIVE PRODUCERS	John C. Ching, Deborah Lau, and Ron Bozman
EXECUTIVE PRODUCERS	Tino Puri and Rohit Khattar
EXECUTIVE PRODUCERS	Stewart Till, Anthony Buckner, and Greg Strasburg
DIRECTOR OF PHOTOGRAPHY	Stuart Dryburgh A.S.C.
PRODUCTION DESIGNER	Mark Friedberg
MUSIC COMPOSED BY	Elliot Goldenthal
EDITOR	Françoise Bonnot A.C.E.
COSTUME DESIGNER	Sandy Powell
VISUAL EFFECTS SUPERVISOR	Kyle Cooper
ARTISTIC ADVISOR / WATER PHOTOGRAPHY	Brian Oglesbee
STILL PHOTOGRAPHER	Melinda Sue Gordon, SMPSP
COLORIST	Yvan Lucas
ASSOCIATE EDITOR	Bob Allen
ASSOCIATE PRODUCER	Phyllis Lavoie
CO-PRODUCER	Nalini Lalvani

CAST

PROSPERA	Helen Mirren
TRINCULO	Russell Brand
FERDINAND	Reeve Carney
GONZALO	Tom Conti
ANTONIO	Chris Cooper
SEBASTIAN	Alan Cumming
CALIBAN	Djimon Hounsou
MIRANDA	Felicity Jones
STEPHANO	Alfred Molina
ALONSO	David Strathairn
ARIEL	Ben Whishaw
BOATSWAIN	Jude Akuwidike

SPECIAL THANKS

Jeffrey Horowitz (Theatre For A New Audience), Bart Walker, Glen Berger, Daria Polichetti, Bill Feightner,
Adam Young and Joe Matza (eFilm), Jules Cazedessus, Sean Cameron Guest, and Katrina Whalen

INTERIOR DESIGNER: Emily Lessard
CASE DESIGNER: Kara Strubel
ART DIRECTOR: Michelle Ishay
PRODUCTION MANAGER: Jules Thomson

Library of Congress Cataloging-in-Publication Data

Taymor, Julie, 1952-
  The tempest / Julie Taymor ; adapted from the play by William
Shakespeare.
— 1st ed.
    p. cm.
  Includes bibliographical references and index.
  ISBN 978-0-8109-9655-7 (alk. paper)
  1. Shakespeare, William, 1564-1616—Film adaptations. I.
Shakespeare,
William, 1564-1616. Tempest. II. Tempest (Motion picture : 2010)
III. Title.
  PN1997.T3853T39 2010
  791.43'6—dc22

                                            0014046

Published in 2010 by Abrams, an imprint of ABRAMS, Inc.

Printed and bound in Hong Kong, China
10 9 8 7 6 5 4 3 2 1

Abrams books are available at special discounts when purchased
in quantity for premiums and promotions as well as fundraising or
educational use. Special editions can also be created to specification.
For details, contact specialmarkets@abramsbooks.com or the
address below.

ABRAMS
THE ART OF BOOKS SINCE 1949
115 West 18th Street
New York, NY 10011
www.abramsbooks.com

PHOTO CREDITS

Melinda Sue Gordon: 12-13, 14, 15, 16, 17, 18 (all), 19 (left), 20 (right), 21
(all), 22 (top right and bottom row), 34, 35, 42, 47, 55, 58, 60, 61, 64-65,
66-67, 70, 71, 74, 75, 78, 79, 80, 82-83, 84, 85, 87, 92, 93, 95, 96-97,
101, 107 (right), 110, 114, 115 (both), 118-119, 130, 131, 133, 134, 137, 152,
154, 155, 158, 166 (left), 167, 172-173

Prologue Films: 19 (right)

Universal Pictures: 20 (left)

Katrina Whalen: 20 (center)